For Jaime — ...VE THINKER

Wishing you all the best on your dangerous journey through the institution. I'm proud of you.

Mark

Legal Education and the
Reproduction of Hierarchy

CRITICAL AMERICA
General Editors: Richard Delgado and Jean Stefancic

White by Law:
The Legal Construction of Race
Ian F. Haney López

Cultivating Intelligence:
Power, Law, and the Politics of Teaching
Louise Harmon and Deborah W. Post

Privilege Revealed:
How Invisible Preference
Undermines America
Stephanie M. Wildmand with Margalynne
Armstrong, Adrienne D. Davis, and Trina
Grillo

Does the Law Morally Bind the Poor? or
What Good's the Constitution When You
Can't Afford a Loaf of Bread?
R. George Wright

Hybrid: Bisexuals, Multiracials, and Other
Misfits under American Law
Ruth Colker

Critical Race Feminism: A Reader
Edited by Adrien Katherine Wing

Immigrants Out!
The New Nativism and the
Anti-Immigrant Impulse
in the United States
Edited by Juan F. Perea

Taxing America
Edited by Karen B. Brown and Mary Louise
Fellows

Notes of a Racial Caste Baby:
Color Blindness and the
End of Affirmative Action
Bryan K. Fair

Please Don't Wish Me a Merry
Christmas: A Critical History of the
Separation of Church and State
Stephen M. Feldman

To Be an American: Cultural Pluralism
and the Rhetoric of Assimilation
Bill Ong Hing

Negrophobia and Reasonable Racism:
The Hidden Costs of Being
Black in America
Jody David Armour

Black and Brown in America:
The Case for Cooperation
Bill Piatt

Black Rage Confronts the Law
Paul Harris

Selling Words:
Free Speech in a Commercial Culture
R. George Wright

The Color of Crime: Racial Hoaxes,
White Fear, Black Protectionism,
Police Harassment, and
Other Macroaggressions
Katheryn K. Russell

The Smart Culture:
Society, Intelligence, and Law
Robert L. Hayman, Jr.

Was Blind, But Now I See:
White Race Consciousness and the Law
Barbara J. Flagg

The Gender Line:
Men, Women, and the Law
Nancy Levit

Heretics in the Temple:
Americans Who Reject
the Nation's Legal Faith
David Ray Papke

The Empire Strikes Back: Outsiders and
the Struggle over Legal Education
Arthur Austin

*Interracial Justice: Conflict and
Reconciliation in
Post–Civil Rights America*
Eric K. Yamamoto

*Black Men on Race, Gender, and
Sexuality: A Critical Reader*
Edited by Devon Carbado

*When Sorry Isn't Enough:
The Controversy over Apologies and Reparations for Human Injustice*
Edited by Roy L. Brooks

*Disoriented: Asian Americans, Law,
and the Nation State*
Robert S. Chang

Rape and the Culture of the Courtroom
Andrew E. Taslitz

The Passions of Law
Edited by Susan A. Bandes

*Global Critical Race Feminism:
An International Reader*
Edited by Adrien Katherine Wing

Law and Religion: Critical Essays
Edited by Stephen M. Feldman

*Changing Race: Latinos, the Census, and
the History of Ethnicity*
Clara E. Rodríguez

*From the Ground Up: Environmental
Racism and the Rise of the
Environmental Justice Movement*
Luke Cole and Sheila Foster

*Nothing but the Truth: Why Trial Lawyers
Don't, Can't, and Shouldn't Have to Tell
the Whole Truth*
Steven Lubet

Critical Race Theory: An Introduction
Richard Delgado and Jean Stefancic

*Playing It Safe: How the Supreme Court
Sidesteps Hard Cases*
Lisa A. Kloppenberg

*Why Lawsuits Are Good for America: Disciplined Democracy, Big Business, and the
Common Law*
Carl T. Bogus

*How the Left Can Win Arguments and
Influence People: A Tactical Manual for
Pragmatic Progressives*
John K. Wilson

*Aftermath:
The Clinton Impeachment and the Presidency in the Age of Political Spectacle*
Edited by Leonard V. Kaplan
and Beverly I. Moran

*Getting over Equality: A Critical Diagnosis
of Religious Freedom in America*
Steven D. Smith

*Critical Race Narratives: A Study of Race,
Rhetoric, and Injury*
Carl Gutiérrez-Jones

*Social Scientists for Social Justice:
Making the Case against Segregation*
John P. Jackson, Jr.

*Victims in the War on Crime:
The Use and Abuse of Victims' Rights*
Markus Dirk Dubber

*Original Sin:
Clarence Thomas and the Failure
of the Constitutional Conservatives*
Samuel A. Marcosson

*Policing Hatred: Law Enforcement, Civil
Rights, and Hate Crime*
Jeannine Bell

*Destructive Messages:
How Hate Speech Paves the Way for
Harmful Social Movements*
Alexander Tsesis

*Moral Imperialism:
A Critical Anthology*
Edited by Berta Esperanza
Hernández-Truyol

In the Silicon Valley of Dreams:
Environmental Injustice,
Immigrant Workers, and the
High-Tech Global Economy
David N. Pellow and
Lisa Sun-Hee Park

Mixed Race America and the Law:
A Reader
Kevin R. Johnson

Critical Race Feminism:
A Reader, Second Edition
Edited by Adrien Katherine Wing

Murder and the Reasonable Man:
Passion and Fear in the
Criminal Courtroom
Cynthia K. Lee

Success without Victory:
Lost Legal Battles and the
Long Road to Justice in America
Jules Lobel

Greasers and Gringos: Latinos, Law, and
the American Imagination
Steven W. Bender

Saving Our Children
from the First Amendment
Kevin W. Saunders

Elusive Citizenship:
Immigration, Asian Americans,
and the Paradox of Civil Rights
John S. W. Park

Truth, Autonomy, and Speech:
Feminist Theory and the
First Amendment
Susan H. Williams

Legal Education and the Reproduction of
Hierarchy: A Polemic against the System:
A Critical Edition
Duncan Kennedy, with commentaries by
Paul Carrington, Peter Gabel, Angela Harris
and Donna Maeda, and Janet Halley

Legal Education and the Reproduction of Hierarchy

A Polemic against the System

A CRITICAL EDITION

Duncan Kennedy

WITH COMMENTARIES BY
Paul Carrington, Peter Gabel,
Angela Harris and Donna Maeda, and Janet Halley

WITH AN INTRODUCTION AND AFTERWORD BY THE AUTHOR

New York University Press

NEW YORK AND LONDON

NEW YORK UNIVERSITY PRESS
New York and London
www.nyupress.org

Library of Congress Cataloging-in-Publication Data
Kennedy, Duncan, 1942–
Legal education and the reproduction of hierarchy :
a polemic against the system : a critical edition
Duncan Kennedy, with commentaries by Paul Carrington . . . [et al.].
p. cm. — (Critical America)
"With an introduction and afterword by the author."
ISBN 0–8147–4778–7 (cloth : alk. paper)
1. Law—Study and teaching—United States.
I. Carrington, Paul. II. Title. III. Series.
KF272.K46   2004
340'.071'173—dc22   2004044990

New York University Press books are printed on acid-free paper,
and their binding materials are chosen for strength and durability.

Manufactured in the United States of America

10 9 8 7 6 5 4 3 2 1

Contents

Introduction   1
  Duncan Kennedy

Legal Education and the Reproduction of Hierarchy:
A Polemic against the System   9
  Duncan Kennedy

Reproducing the Right Sort of Hierarchy   145
  Paul Carrington

The Spiritual Foundation of Attachment to Hierarchy   154
  Peter Gabel

Power and Resistance in Contemporary Legal Education   168
  Angela Harris and Donna Maeda

Of Time and the Pedagogy of Critical Legal Studies   185
  Janet Halley

Afterword   202
  Duncan Kennedy

About the Contributors   223

Introduction

Duncan Kennedy

Legal Education and the Reproduction of Hierarchy: A Polemic against the System was published (self-published) as a pamphlet in 1983. Over the next ten years or so, I gave away or sold (through the Harvard Book Store in Cambridge or "mail order") about three thousand copies. The readers were law students and law teachers. In retrospect, they seem to have been drawn to one or more of the following aspects of the book. Starting from a very negative view of American life, it offers an analysis of how legal education participates in the production of what sucks about the system. It does this partly through a novelistic, subjective evocation of the social-psychological pressures that work to make entering students into lawyers and citizens who will participate willingly in the reproduction of the system, making it seem like something natural. The book proposes a radical egalitarian alternative vision of what legal education should become, and a strategy, starting from the anarchist idea of workplace organizing, for struggle in that direction.

The New York University Press Critical America series has graciously agreed to reproduce the book in its original pamphlet form in this reprint, with commentary by Paul Carrington, Peter Gabel, Angela Harris and Donna Maeda, and Janet Halley, and an Afterword. In the Afterword, I attempt to situate the pamphlet, describing how I came to write and publish it in its peculiar form and where it fits in the history of Critical Legal Studies. The pamphlet was addressed to first-year law students who had what we then vaguely called "progressive" sympathies. Its audience is the same today. I have at least a sense of who it appeals to, because I still teach in the first year, and some of my students have managed to get a hold of it even though I long since stopped selling it. In this Introduction, I try to give a picture of who its audience seems to be.

In my first-year Torts course, I use a casebook but also photocopied materials that teach the same rules the other sections cover, but through cases that raise gender, race, and class issues. As I face the class of eighty-five students, they seem only half aware that I am watching them at the same time that they are watching me. Sometimes I catch a look, a fleeting expression hidden from the other students in the room, on the face of a student listening to another student, maybe in the next seat over. The look says, "I can't believe he (or she) just said that."

Sometimes it's surprised, sometimes disgusted; sometimes there is a shrug of contemptuous familiarity. The remark that provokes the look won't be overtly racist or homophobic or anti-Muslim. It is that the class's discussion of the race or class or gender or religious issue comes from deep in the "mainstream," so deep that it is just assumed that being hit on by another man would naturally really really freak you out, or that abused women should just leave their husbands, or that poor people have an unfortunate tendency to financial irresponsibility. The students for whom these mainstream moments are alienating don't realize how many other students in the room are alienated too, or will be alienated when the topic shifts to another enraging cliché. There are even socially conservative students who are feeling the same thing from the other side: "Where *am* I?"

I have my own rough categories to describe potential resisters, although I am constantly surprised that people who "should" don't, and that people who you'd never expect to be radicals turn out to be just that. For example, there are people who are in law school looking to do international human rights work. Often they've traveled abroad, independently, between college and law school, rather than going to work as a paralegal in a big city law firm the way everyone else did. They are very aware that the world is full of extreme poverty and brutal oppression, by states and by cultures, of the poor, of children, of women, of dissenters, of minorities of all kinds. And they are aware that in the United States, we either ignore it or sense that it is the fault of the people who suffer it, that we rich Americans are absolutely and unequivocally not implicated ourselves. In the rest of the world, it is clear to just about everyone that we are implicated, or even ultimately responsible. For some students in this group, international human rights means an unbudgeable commitment to victims because they are "the other." For children of the African American, Latino/a, Asian American, or Arab American middle class, the same commitment can be motivated by the possibility or reality that the sufferers are close or very distant relatives.

Another, maybe overlapping category includes people who have thought, from high school on, that there is a lot that is vicious in the way the boys treat the girls (not that the girls are necessarily always innocent)—people who know something about stalking or rape or sexual harassment or sex work, who have worked in a shelter. The class discussion seems out of a fifties sitcom, combining "none of this could ever happen to me" naïveté among the women, especially the cocky conservative women, and a too-sharp eye out for political correctness from even the liberal men. You might be the only out lesbian in the class, or the only closeted lesbian you know in the class, and not believe for a minute that the norm of nondiscrimination that everyone claims to believe in will stop them from treating you differently when they think of you as gay.

There are children of African American or Latino/a professionals or small-business people, wary of the overwhelming whiteness of the milieu, determined to master it by working like a dog. Mainstreamers speak as though everyone comes from a middle-class white suburb or a gentrified urban neighborhood. The all-black community and the barrio are alien and invisible to them. Perhaps they are alien to you as well, but not invisible, never completely outside consciousness; something to which you have a connection, like it or not. The idea is to take advantage of the reality of opportunity while somehow getting past the implicit humiliations of affirmative action, avoid appearing to be an "angry black," hoping that a really outrageous, denigrating stereotype about your community won't force you into the fray, and then to "give back."

Studying "theory" in college, meaning any kind of postmodern critical stance—Cultural Studies, perhaps—might be a route to resistance. But it often seems to disable rather than empower in the first year law school classroom, because teachers and fellow students are exactly the people whose ideas and whole way of thinking you have rejected and gotten beyond. Two students in a class of a hundred have even heard the names Foucault or Derrida. The teacher has heard the names, period. If the theoretically sophisticated student decides to stick with what seemed the blinding illuminations of college, she will have to deconstruct law *starting from scratch all by herself*. All that is solid melts into air, you learned, but your four casebooks weigh fifteen pounds. You studied privileging, hegemony, the subaltern, silencing, and now that is you, not in your identity-politics identity but in your po-mo identity.

There are also the first American-born children of professional-class immigrants from countries where politics, religious and ideological, is a deadly business, and people know and care about it in a way that seems eerily absent here. Perhaps the parents are secular Muslims. Or the student might have grown up in the Iranian post-Pahlevi cosmopolitan diaspora, or in a small town in the Middle West where a Catholic Tamil father was the only doctor. "White" test scores got you into the Ivy League where your dark skin caused you to be mistaken for a burglar trying to rob your dorm. These students aren't bound by whatever Cuba or Vietnam or Lebanon meant to their parents, but the simple-minded or repressive parochialism of the mainstream, especially after 9/11, has no place for them. On the other hand, your parents may think an arranged marriage would be the perfect way to celebrate a graduate degree.

"The sixties" is present in the law school classroom through children marked by their parents who were marked by their times. Parents who were radicals, hippies, veterans, civil rights workers, musicians, poverty workers, social workers on reservations, Peace Corps volunteers. For their children, the question is whether to turn from their parents' ghosts, or to live their parents' lives right this time, or to do the opposite this time. The parents are often Jewish and/or WASP, or of different races, divorced sometime in the eighties as the tallest divorce wave in American history hit, and the sexual revolution crashed, and married men came out and left their wives, and the AIDS epidemic got under way. Your mother raised and pushed and supported you, but she also needed your support in return, big time. Your father was gone or dead or just never recovered from Vietnam or from his brother's descent into schizophrenia. Maybe you lived in the country, without electricity and with water hand-drawn from a well, and now find yourself tossed up on the shore of middle-class lawyer success in a kind of daze, given what it was all like just a few years ago. Worried about betraying those fragile forebears, worried about betraying the universe of people you have been a part of but that your fellow classmates treat as more remote than Afghanis. Also worried about having been betrayed, perhaps crippled, by the strangeness of the childhood they inflicted.

These types aren't mutually exclusive, of course. One thing that binds them together is that for many resisting students, not just the children of sixties parents, it turns out that there is something in the past that is marking or scarring or revelatory, involving mental illness, disability, crime, alcoholism, drug addiction, AIDS, suicide, domestic abuse or other violence at close range, displacement, abandonment, frequent changes of school, poverty in the midst of plenty, or relative wealth amid crushing poverty, something that somehow set the person apart in the crowd, in his or her own mind, and at the same time aligned him or her with the crowd of the lost and injured and oppressed.

The same may be true of mainstream students, but they have managed, for good or ill, to move on or deny. They are preoccupied with their careers, with getting a job, making money, getting married, deciding where to live—getting through law school as trade school, with no intellectual, political, cultural agenda of any kind for their legal education, on the way to life in the mainstream afterward. The dominant student culture is Middle American on both coasts as well as in the middle. It is closer to jock or fraternity culture than to nerd or cool-people culture.

Mainstreamers are aware that there are others than themselves, namely the conservative students, growing more self-confident every year, more and more willing to challenge the liberal elements in the mainstream's cliché-ridden discourse and to jump on anything that smells of political correctness, just as the politically correct once jumped on them. They are divided between social conservatives and libertarian conservatives, allied in law school in the Federalist Society. The scary ones are the right-wing econ jocks, who've studied some form of conservative economics in college, or business or finance or accounting, or even have master's degrees. They intimidate the liberals in the mainstream.

If you are on the invisible other side of the mainstream, you are likely to be a humanist, maybe even an artist, maybe a numerophobe, or a person with a solid contempt for the cultural and intellectual style of right-wing youth. Contempt can suddenly turn to dust when you realize what a massive advantage the econ jocks have, that the teacher is almost as scared of them as you are, and that there is absolutely no way you are going to be able to catch up. The school isn't going to help, and the econ jocks themselves certainly aren't going to either.

Then there are the gunners, the students who talk all the time, pursue the teacher after class, brutally try to upstage or cut out their fellow students. Gunners can be a major obsession or a minor annoyance. They are violating a norm held by everyone in the class: the norm of not grabbing. Many students react with "projective identification"—directing at the gunners all the loathing they feel for the part of themselves that they are barely managing to restrain, in obedience to the norm, from doing the same and maybe worse. The gunners can also be really intimidating, suggesting that there is a level of understanding of the material and an ability to talk the talk that the silent listeners will never achieve.

The faculty, although only occasionally obnoxious, are not much help. They are bland politically, concealing any passionate commitments, except that maybe once in a semester they will get exercised about a case and "break role" for an instant to let you know just how strongly they feel that it should have come out for the sympathetic losing party. They show their colors by becoming advisers to particular student organizations, or maybe by coming to hear (or themselves bringing in) an outside speaker with an overt liberal political agenda. They are better or worse, technically, professionally, in their clearly defined mission of helping you learn what they are teaching, which is just what everyone else is teaching except about a different particular doctrinal area. Some make it clear; some don't seem to be able to.

You may sense that they have dropped out of the world you're entering and that they are delighted not to have to do what you will have to do. Along with, or instead, of their bar admission certificates, they have family pictures and their children's paintings on their office walls, announcing things they care deeply about (one doubts they have students' pictures on the walls at home), things they are spending a lot more time on than you will be able to for many associate years to come. They are helping you adjust to that reality rather than resist it. There is the occasional leftover sixties person who vaguely suggests that you and your whole generation are not up to whatever it is that they were, but no longer are, up to.

If you are a potential resister, a way to give a modicum of meaning to all of this is to keep in mind that progressive lawyers do things that are interesting and ethical and political in every area of American life. They are a saving remnant. In law school, there is typically a public interest coalition generating a diffuse commonality across the different categories of resistance, and including the liberal activist part of the mainstream. Extracurricular organizations, journals, and clinics can be enclaves. If you want a long-term life project that works against loss and injury and oppression, going to law school is a way to find it. And it is worth remembering that it is not only jobs overtly associated with the public interest that count. Private law firms make money doing anti-discrimination and sexual harassment law, and the much-reviled "plaintiffs' bar" is actually the main force behind consumer protection in our country.

The drawback of this strategy is that it means treating three years of your life as a mere interim. Focusing forward to a job and inward to family and sideways to a nonacademic community, however defined, means passing up the chance to experiment with resistance to the system while you are still relatively autonomous within it. If you are an activist, you choose your area of activity based on your identity. You do women's issues only if you are a woman, civil rights or poverty or criminal justice issues if you are black or Latino/a, living wage or sweatshops if you are Asian American or have some working-class identification, gay rights if you are gay, international human rights if you are third world–identified, environmentalism or the death penalty sometimes just because you can do them, as a liberal, middle-class white person, without having to apologize for your privileges all the time.

It would be a good idea to find a way to hook up with one another and kick against the traces in the present—by analyzing and protesting *inside law school, against law school.* I had a better idea of how that might work, in student-faculty coalitions, in 1983 than I do now. But I don't feel that the opportunities for oppositionism are smaller now than they were then. Resistance is an attitude that turns into an activity, that becomes a habit, and pretty soon it's like the habit of exercise and you feel bored and unused when you aren't making trouble for someone somehow. The spiritual dimension of resistance is nonetheless positive. It is about the ecstatic moment of finding other risk takers, making plans, arguing all night long about what to do, doing something.

My sense is that the first steps I describe in the later parts of this book still have a lot to be said for them. An essential preliminary is to work against the sense that each of the identities I described above is uniquely victimized, uniquely isolated, unintelligible to all the others. In other words, I'm for some postmodernism-inspired rebellion against identity politics, not in the name of assimilation to the mainstream but in the name of a large countercultural project—cosmopolitan and original rather than inward-turning or backward-looking. In any case, it seems as certain as anything can ever be that the time of analysis and protest will come around again; that many people my age won't recognize it but some will, with cheers, as it clears the bend in the road on its way toward us; and that it will be *new.*

Cambridge, Mass.
July 2003

LEGAL EDUCATION

AND THE REPRODUCTION OF

HIERARCHY

A POLEMIC AGAINST THE SYSTEM

Duncan Kennedy

A F A R
CAMBRIDGE
1 9 8 3

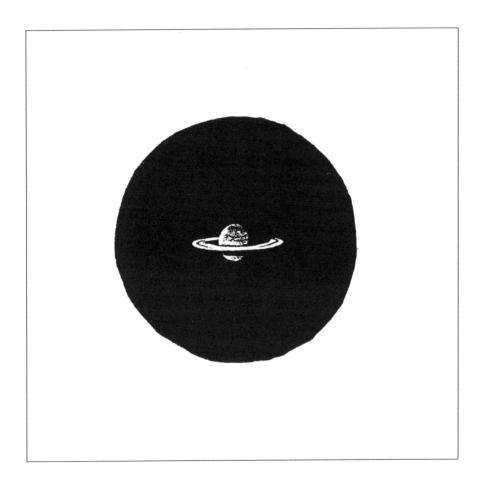

LEGAL EDUCATION AND THE
REPRODUCTION OF HIERARCHY

A Polemic Against the System

Duncan Kennedy

Afar
Cambridge
1983

Parts of Chapter 1 and Chapters 2, 5 and 6 of this essay first appeared in The Politics of Law: A Progressive Critique, David Kairys, ed., Pantheon 1982 (under the title "Legal Education as Training for Hierarchy"). Another short version appeared in 32 J. Leg. Ed. 591 (1982).

First Edition, Sixth Printing, May 1984

From Beatrix Potter, The Tale of Two Bad Mice (Warne 1908)

Contents

Preface

1. The First Year Experience

2. The Ideological Content of Legal Education

3. Hierarchies of the Legal Profession

4. The Contribution of Legal Education to the Hierarchies of the Bar

5. The Modeling of Hierarchical Relationships

6. The Student Response to Hierarchy

7. The Politics of Hierarchy

8. Strategy

9. The Law School Study Group

Utopian Proposal

Reading List

From Beatrix Potter, The Tale of Two Bad Mice (Warne 1908)

Preface

This is an essay about the role of legal education in American social life. It is a description of the ways in which legal education contributes to the reproduction of illegitimate hierarchy in the bar and in society. And it suggests ways in which left students and teachers who are determined not to let law school demobilize them can make the experience part of a left activist practice of social transformation.

The general thesis is that law schools are intensely poli- tical places, in spite of the fact that they seem intellectually unpretentious, barren of theoretical ambition or practical vision of what social life might be. The trade school mentality, the endless attention to trees at the expense of forests, the alter- nating grimness and chumminess of focus on the limited task at hand, all these are only a part of what is going on. The other part is ideological training for willing service in the hier- archies of the corporate welfare state.

To say that law school is ideological is to say that what teachers teach along with basic skills is wrong, is nonsense about what law is and how it works. It is to say that the mes- sage about the nature of legal competence, and its distribution among students, is wrong, is nonsense. It is to say that the

i

ideas about the possibilities of life as a lawyer that students pick up from legal education are wrong, are nonsense. But all this is nonsense with a tilt, it is biased and motivated rather than random error. What it says is that it is natural, efficient and fair for law firms, the bar as a whole, and the society the bar services to be organized in their actual patterns of hierarchy and domination.

Because most students believe what they are told, explicitly and implicitly, about the world they are entering, they behave in ways that fulfill the prophecies the system makes about them and about that world. This is the link-back that completes the system: students do more than accept the way things are, and ideology does more than damp opposition. Students act affirmatively within the channels cut for them, cutting them deeper, giving the whole a patina of consent, and weaving complicity into everyone's life story.

Resist!

ii

Chapter One

The First Year Experience

A surprisingly large number of law students go to law school with the notion that being a lawyer means something more, something more socially constructive than just doing a highly respectable job.   There is the idea of playing the role an earlier generation associated with Brandeis, the role of service through law, carried out with superb technical competence and also with a deep belief that in its essence law is a progressive force, however much it may be distorted by the actual arrangements of capitalism.   There is a contrasting, more radical notion, that law is a tool of established interests, that it is in essence superstructural, but that it is a tool a coldly effective professional can sometimes turn against the dominators. Whereas in the first notion, the student aspires to help the oppressed and transform society by bringing out the latent content of a valid ideal, in the second, the student sees herself as part technician, part judo expert, able to turn the tables exactly because she never lets herself be mystified by the rhetoric that is so important to other students.

Then there are the conflicting motives, which, I think, are equally real for both types. People think of law school as extremely competitive, as a place where a tough, hard-working, smart style is cultivated and rewarded. Students enter law school with a sense that they will develop that side of themselves. Even if they disapprove, on principle, of that side of themselves, they have had other experiences in which it turned out that they wanted and liked aspects of themselves that on principle they disapproved of. How is one to know that one is not "really" looking to develop oneself in this way as much as one is motivated by the vocation of social transformation?

There is also the issue of social mobility. Almost everyone whose parents were not members of the professional/technical intelligentsia seems to feel that going to law school is an advance, in terms of the family history. This is true even for children of high level business managers, so long as their parents' positions were due to hard work and struggle rather than to birth into the upper echelons. Though there may be sadness or hurt at the implicit rejection of their style of life, it is rare for parents to actively disapprove of their children going to law school, whatever their origins.   So taking this particular step has a social meaning, however much the student may reject it, and that social meaning is success.   The success is bitter-sweet if one feels one should have gotten into a better school, but both the bitter and the sweet suggest that one's motives are impure.

The initial classroom experience sustains rather than dissipates ambivalence.   The teachers are overwhelmingly white, male, and deadeningly straight and middle class in manner. The classroom is hierarchical with a vengeance, the teacher receiving a degree of deference and arousing fears that remind one of high school rather than college.   The sense of autonomy one has in a lecture, with the rule that you must let teacher drone on without interruption balanced by the rule that teacher can't do anything to you, is gone.   In its place is a demand for a pseudo-participation in which you struggle desperately, in front of a large audience, to read a mind determined to elude you.

It is almost never anything like as bad as The Paper Chase or One-L, but it is still humiliating to be frightened and unsure of oneself, especially when what renders one unsure is a classroom arrangement that suggests at once the patriarchal family and a Kafka-like riddle-state.   The law school classroom at the beginning of the first year is culturally reactionary.

4   Legal Education and the

But it is also engaging. You are learning a new language, and it is possible to learn it. Pseudo-participation makes one intensely aware of how everyone else is doing, providing endless bases for comparison. Information is coming in on all sides, and things that you knew were out there but didn't understand are becoming intelligible. The teacher offers subtle encouragements as well as not so subtle reasons for alarm. Performance is on one's mind, adrenalin flows, success has a nightly and daily meaning in terms of the material assigned. After all, this is the next segment: one is moving from the vaguely sentimental world of college, or the frustrating world of officework or housework, into something that promises a dose of "reality," even if it's cold and scary reality.

It quickly emerges that neither the students nor the faculty are as homogeneous as they at first appeared. Some teachers are more authoritarian than others; some students other than oneself reacted with horror to the infantilization of the first days or weeks. There even seems to be a connection between classroom manner and substantive views, with the "softer" teachers also seeming to be more "liberal," perhaps more sympathetic to plaintiffs in the torts course, more willing to hear what are called policy arguments, as well as less intimidating in class discussion.

There is a disturbing aspect to this process of differentiation: in most law schools, it turns out that the tougher, less

Reproduction of Hierarchy   5

policy-oriented teachers are the more popular. The softies seem to get less matter across, they let things wander, and one begins to worry that their niceness is at the expense of a metaphysical quality called "rigor," thought to be essential to success on bar exams and in the grown-up world of practice. Ambivalence reasserts itself. As between the conservatives and the mushy centrists, enemies who scare you but subtly reassure you may seem more attractive than allies no better anchored than yourself.

There is an intellectual experience that somewhat corresponds to this emotional one. Its theme is that there is no purchase for left or even for committed liberal thinking on any part of the smooth surface of legal education. The issue in the classroom is not left against right, but pedagogical conservatism against moderate, disintegrated liberalism. No one of one's teachers is likely to present a model of either left pedagogy or vital left theoretical enterprise, though some <u>are</u> likely to be vaguely sympathetic to progressive causes and <u>some</u> may even be moonlighting as left lawyers. Students are struggling for cognitive mastery, and against the sneaking depression of the pre-professional.

The actual intellectual content of the law seems to consist of learning rules, what they are and why they have to be the way they are, while rooting for the occasional judge who seems willing to make them marginally more humane. The basic ex-

6   Legal Education and the

perience is of double surrender: to a passivizing classroom
experience and to a passive attitude toward the content of the
legal system.

The first step toward this sense of the irrelevance of
liberal or left thinking is the opposition in the first year curriculum between the technical, boring, difficult, obscure legal
case, and the occasional case with outrageous facts and a pig-
gish judicial opinion endorsing or tolerating the outrage. The
first kind of case--call it a cold case--is a challenge to interest, understanding, even to wakefulness. It can be on any
subject, so long as it is of no political or moral or emotional
significance. Just to understand what happened and what's
being said about it, you have to learn a lot of new terms, a
little potted legal history, and lots of rules, none of which is
carefully explained by the casebook or the teacher. It is difficult to figure out why the case is there in the first place,
difficult to figure out whether one has grasped it, and difficult to anticipate what the teacher will ask and what one
should respond.

The other kind of case usually involves a sympathetic
plaintiff, say an Appalachian farm family, and an unsympa-
thetic defendant, say a coal company. On first reading, it
appears that the coal company has screwed the farm family,
say by renting their land for strip mining, with a promise to
restore it to its original condition once the coal has been ex-

tracted, and then reneging on the promise. And the case should include a judicial opinion that does something like awarding a meaningless couple of hundred dollars to the farm family, rather than making the coal company do the restoration work.

The point of the class discussion will be that your initial reaction of outrage is naive, non-legal, irrelevant to what you're supposed to be learning, and maybe substantively wrong into the bargain. There are good reasons for the awful result, when you take a legal and logical view, as opposed to a knee-jerk passionate view, and if you can't muster those reasons, maybe you aren't cut out to be a lawyer.

Here is a description of a class in civil procedure given at a reputable West Coast law school during the first week of the school year. The subject was a case in a U.S. Court of Appeal. In the trial court, plaintiff had succeeded in establishing jurisdiction on the basis of diversity of citizenship. But he lost on the merits. On appeal, he attacked his own earlier position on diversity, and persuaded the appellate court to reverse the defendant's lower court judgment for want of jurisdiction.

The teacher brought out early in the discussion that the plaintiff would be able, after the dismissal of the federal case, to bring suit in the state court. Members of the class pro-

posed several reasons why plaintiff might want to do this:
maybe the appellate court was unlikely to reverse the trial
court on the merits, whereas there was some chance of winning
in the state court; perhaps plaintiff's counsel had realized that
even if they won in the appellate court, the Supreme Court
was sure to reverse on jurisdictional or other grounds.

The teacher then elicited reasons to be shocked by the
outcome. It was wasteful in terms of judicial resources to try
the case de novo in the state court. It was a strain and expense to the defendant to have to defend himself twice. It
was patently unfair to allow the party who had initially argued
for diversity jurisdiction to turn around, after losing on the
merits, and argue the other side. The possible incompetence
of plaintiff's counsel was being rewarded rather than punished.

The teacher laid great and dramatic emphasis on all these
aspects of the situation, suggesting that the rule of law allowing the jurisdictional challenge by plaintiff on appeal was
"wrong," "irrational," "stupid," designed to enrich lawyers
and impoverish litigants, and so on. But the denunciations
were in the form of questions: "Can it be?" "What possible
explanation is there?" "Are you trying to tell me that the
system is that badly organized?" The teacher structured the
situation as a puzzle. The students were to look for an answer
in the text of the appellate court opinion.

   Some students volunteered that the case was just wrongly decided, for the reasons just mentioned. The teacher referred to this response as "equity above all," "justice no matter what the cost." It was clear that it was inadequate, and implicit that students who proposed it suffered from an excessive, non-legal concern with the particular fact situation.

   Other students argued, in the other direction, that "jurisdiction is jurisdiction," so that the federal courts "simply lacked power" to decide the case. This response was also excoriated, on the ground that it elevated "legal technicalities" above "substance." Moreover, the teacher pointed out that so long as the case was before the Court of Appeal, it was meaningless to say there was "no power." If the court decided it on the merits, there was no one to say it nay, except the U.S. Supreme Court. Here also there was a strong implicit message: that the law is not a matter of conceptual juggling, and that mere words decide nothing.

   Students attempting to resolve the dilemma started various digressions into the more obscure passages in the opinion. In the course of disposing of these false leads, the teacher imparted a lot of information about the basic operations of the procedural system. At the end of the hour, the class was still hunting for something in the text that would adequately explain the outcome without resort either to the particular equities or to formalism. The level of tension and excited frustration was high.

As people began to assemble their books and papers, the teacher went back to several earlier comments he had seemed to dismiss. He pointed out that responding in an equitable way to this case would raise a host of practical difficulties and require a large number of doctrinal complexities. Suppose we adopt a rule that you can't attack jurisdiction on appeal if you argued for it below. What if no one had even questioned jurisdiction below? If, in such a case, the plaintiff could challenge it on appeal (but couldn't if he had discussed the issue) there would be a perverse incentive not to discuss tricky jurisdictional problems. What would be the precedential effect of the appellate court refusing to question jurisdiction in a case like this one? The teacher's tone suggested that these questions were unanswerable.

In short, there were great advantages to having a clean, certain rule knowable in advance. Such a rule would eliminate any incentive for either party to treat the jurisdiction issue lightly, since either might have any gains on the merits wiped out by the other party on appeal. Over the long run, there would be fewer inequities if the appellate court took a very strong and severe stand rather than adopting a confusing and uncertain ad hoc approach.

The teacher then proposed a second, more surprising argument. The issue in the case was the "integrity of federalism." If the appellate court could not look at the jurisdictional issue on appeal, the parties, in cahoots with compliant lower level federal judges, would be able to encroach on the sphere of the state courts. More and more cases would end up in the national system, with the result that there would be resentment and ill feeling along with atrophy of indigenous in- stitutions.

In conclusion, according to the teacher, there were "important and legitimate interests," federalism on the one hand and overall, long run efficiency on the other, that sup- ported the rule. This in spite of its apparent inequity in the particular case. The students wrote furiously for a few moments, and then got up and left.

Several students described this class to me as "brilliant" and "useful," contrasting it with vaguer, more "policy- oriented" or "theoretical" classroom discussions. They saw the teacher as producing truth about a complicated, important practical problem. They had been anxious that this class, like some others they had attended, would end with a sense that the problem was not just insoluble but hopelessly confusing, and that they would have learned nothing. They were de- lighted that it hadn't turned out that way.

They accepted the teacher's solution without any real questioning in part just because he <u>was</u> the teacher, master of the technical mystery of legal reasoning. But they were also

12   Legal Education and the

substantively satisfied: it seemed plausible that you sometimes have to have harsh but clear general rules for the sake of efficiency, and that federalism sometimes requires the sacrifice of justice in the particular case.

In fact, the teacher's solution was neither intellectually powerful nor well presented. There were familiar arguments in favor of equity in the particular case that he just ignored; his federalism argument was obscure if it made any sense at all. What he offered was not substance, but a spurious sense of closure in a situation in which leaving things open leaves students panicky.

The particular mode of closure had a strong implicit message something like this: "Behind legal outcomes that appear unfair or sinister there is likely to be a highly rational explanation. It is the job of the student to find this explanation. It will be couched in legal reasoning that appeals to general social purposes requiring a particular outcome rather than to situational equities (formalistic mumbo-jumbo is just as bad as mere equity)."

Most students can't fight the combination of cold cases and hot cases. The cold cases are boring, but you have to do them if you want to become a lawyer. The hot cases cry out for response, seem to say that if you can't respond you've already sold out, but the system tells you to put away childish

Reproduction of Hierarchy   13

things, and your reaction to the hot cases is one of them. Without any intellectual resources, in the way of knowledge of the legal system and of the character of legal reasoning, it will appear that emoting will only isolate and incapacitate you. The choice is to develop some calluses and hit the books, or admit failure almost before you've begun.

Chapter Two

The Ideological Content of Legal Education

One can distinguish in a rough way between two aspects of legal education as a reproducer of hierarchy. A lot of what happens is the inculcation through the formal curriculum and the classroom experience of a set of political attitudes toward the economy and society in general, toward law, and toward the possibilities of life in the profession. These have a general ideological significance, and they have an impact on the lives even of law students who never practice law. Then there is a complicated set of institutional practices that orient students to willing participation in the specialized hierarchical roles of lawyers. In order to understand these, one must have at least a rough conception of what the world of practice is like.

Reproduction of Hierarchy   15

Students begin to absorb the more general ideological message before they have much in the way of a conception of life after law school, so I will describe this formal aspect of the educational process first. I will then try to sketch in the realities of professional life that students gradually learn about in the second and third year, before describing the way in which the institutional practices of law schools bear on those realities.

Law students sometimes speak as though they learned nothing in school. In fact, they learn skills, to do a list of simple but important things. They learn to retain large numbers of rules organized into categorical systems (requisites for a contract, rules about breach, etc.). They learn "issue spotting," which means identifying the ways in which the rules are ambiguous, in conflict, or have a gap when applied to particular fact situations. They learn elementary case analysis, meaning the art of generating broad holdings for cases, so they will apply beyond their intuitive scope, and narrow holdings for cases, so that they won't apply where it at first seemed they would. And they learn a list of balanced, formulaic, pro/con policy arguments that lawyers use in arguing that a given rule should apply to a situation, in spite of a gap, conflict or ambiguity, or that a given case should be extended or narrowed. These are arguments like "the need for certainty," and "the need for flexibility;" "the need to promote competition," and the "need to encourage production by letting producers keep the rewards of their labor."

One should neither exalt these skills nor denigrate them. By comparison with the first year student's tendency to flip-flop between formalism and mere equitable intuition, they represent a real intellectual advance. Lawyers actually do use them in practice. And when properly, consciously mastered, they have "critical" bite. They are a help in thinking about politics, public policy, ethical discourse in general, because they show the indeterminacy and manipulability of ideas and institutions that are central to liberalism.

On the other hand, law schools teach these rather rudimentary, essentially instrumental skills in a way that almost completely mystifies them for almost all law students. The mystification has three parts. First, the schools teach skills through class discussions of cases in which it is asserted that law emerges from a rigorous analytical procedure called "legal reasoning," which is unintelligible to the layman, but somehow both explains and validates the great majority of the rules in force in our system. At the same time, the class context and the materials present every legal issue as distinct from every other, as a tub on its own bottom, so to speak, with no hope or even any reason to hope that from law study one might derive an integrating vision of what law is, how it works, or how it might be changed (other than in an incremental, case by case, reformist way).

Second, the teaching of skills in the mystified context of legal reasoning about utterly unconnected legal problems means that skills are taught badly, unselfconsciously, to be absorbed by osmosis as one picks up the knack of "thinking like a lawyer." Bad or only randomly good teaching generates and then accentuates real differences and imagined differences in student capabilities. But it does so in such a way that students don't know when they are learning and when they aren't, and have no way of improving or even understanding their own learning processes. They experience skills training as the gradual emergence of differences among themselves, as a process of ranking that reflects something that is just "there" inside them.

Third, the schools teach skills in isolation from actual lawyering experience. "Legal reasoning" is sharply distinguished from law practice, and one learns nothing about practice. This procedure disables students from any future role but that of apprentice in a law firm organized in the same manner as a law school, with older lawyers controlling the content and pace of depoliticized craft training in a setting of intense competition and no feedback.

The Formal Curriculum: Legal Rules and Legal Reasoning

The intellectual core of the ideology is the distinction between law and policy. Teachers convince students that legal reasoning exists, and is different from policy analysis, by bullying them into accepting as valid in particular cases arguments about legal correctness that are circular, question-begging, incoherent, or so vague as to be meaningless. Sometimes these are just arguments from authority, with the validity of the authoritative premise put outside discussion by professorial fiat. Sometimes they are policy arguments (security of transaction, business certainty) that are treated in a particular situation as though they were rules that everyone accepts, but that will be ignored in the next case when they would suggest that the decision was wrong. Sometimes they are exercises in formal logic that wouldn't stand up for a minute in a discussion between equals (expectation damages represent the will of the parties).

Within a given subfield, the teacher is likely to treat cases in three different ways. There are the cases that present and justify the basic rules and basic ideas of the field. These are treated as cursory exercises in legal logic. Then there are cases that are anomalous--sometimes they are "outdated," sometimes "wrongly decided" because they don't follow the supposed inner logic of the area. There won't be many of these, but they are important because their treatment persuades students that the technique of legal reasoning is at least minimally independent of the results reached by particular judges, is capable of criticizing as well as legitimating.

Finally, there will be an equally small number of peripheral or "cutting edge" cases the teacher sees as raising policy issues about growth or change in the law. Whereas in discussing the first two kinds of cases the teacher behaves in an authoritarian way supposedly based on his objective knowledge of the technique of legal reasoning, here everything is different. Because we are dealing with "value judgments" that have "political" overtones, the discussion will be much more free-wheeling. Rather than every student comment being right or wrong, all student comments get pluralist acceptance, and the teacher will reveal himself to be either a liberal or a conservative, rather than merely a legal technician.

The curriculum as a whole has a rather similar structure. It is not really a random assortment of tubs on their own bottoms, a forest of tubs. First, there are contracts, torts, property, criminal law and civil procedure. The rules in these courses are the ground-rules of late nineteenth century laissez-faire capitalism. Teachers teach them as though they had an inner logic, as an exercise in legal reasoning with policy (e.g., promissory estoppel in the contracts course) playing a relatively minor role.

Then there are second and third year courses that expound the moderate reformist program of the New Deal and the administrative structure of the modern regulatory state (with passing reference to the racial egalitarianism of the Warren

Court). These courses are more policy oriented than first year courses, and also much more ad hoc. Teachers teach students that limited interference with the market makes sense, and is as authoritatively grounded in statutes as the ground rules of laissez faire are grounded in natural law. But each problem is discrete, enormously complicated, and understood in a way that guarantees the practical impotence of the reform program.

Finally, there are peripheral subjects, like legal philosophy or legal history, legal process, clinical legal education. These are presented as not truly relevant to the "hard" objective, serious, rigorous analytic core of law. They are a kind of playground or a finishing school for learning the social art of self-presentation as a lawyer.

This whole body of implicit messages is nonsense. Legal reasoning is not distinct, as a method for reaching correct results, from ethical and political discourse in general (i.e., from policy analysis). It is true that there is a distinctive lawyers' body of knowledge of the rules in force. It is true that there are distinctive lawyers' argumentative techniques for spotting gaps, conflicts and ambiguities in the rules, for arguing broad and narrow holdings of cases, and for generating pro and con policy arguments. But these are only argumentative techniques. There is never a "correct legal solution" that is other than the correct ethical and political solution to that legal problem.

Reproduction of Hierarchy 21

Put another way, everything taught, except the formal rules themselves and the argumentative techniques for manipulating them, is policy and nothing more. It follows that the classroom distinction between the unproblematic legal case and the policy oriented case is a mere artifact: each could as well be taught in the opposite way. And the curricular distinction between the "nature" of contract law as highly legal and technical by contrast, say, with environmental law, is equally a mystification.

These errors have a bias in favor of the center-liberal program of limited reform of the market economy and pro forma gestures toward racial and sexual equality. The bias arises because law school teaching makes the choice of hierarchy and domination, which is implicit in the adoption of the rules of property, contract and tort, look as though it flows from legal reasoning, rather than from politics and economics. The bias is reenforced when the center-liberal reformist program of regulation is presented as equally authoritative, but somehow more policy oriented, and therefore less fundamental.

The message is that the system is basically OK, since we have patched up the few areas open to abuse, and that it has a limited but important place for value-oriented debate about further change and improvement. If there is to be more fundamental questioning, it is relegated to the periphery of history or philosophy. The real world is kept at bay by treating

clinical legal education, which might bring in a lot of information threatening to the cosy liberal consensus, as free legal
drudge work for the local bar or as mere skills training.

It would be an extraordinary first year student who
could, on his or her own, develop a theoretically critical attitude toward this system.   Entering students just don't know
enough to figure out where the teacher is fudging, misrepre-
senting and otherwise distorting legal thinking and legal reality.   To make matters worse, the two most common kinds of
left thinking the student is likely to bring with her are likely
to hinder rather than assist in the struggle to maintain some
intellectual autonomy from the experience.

Most liberal students believe that the left program can be
reduced to guaranteeing people their rights, and to bringing
about the triumph of human rights over mere property rights.
In this picture, the trouble with the legal system is that it
fails to put the state behind the rights of the oppressed, or
that the system fails to enforce the rights formally recognized.
If one thinks about law this way, one is inescapably dependent
on the very techniques of legal reasoning that are being
marshalled in defense of the status quo.

This wouldn't be so bad if the problem with legal education were that the teachers misused rights reasoning to restrict the range of the rights of the oppressed.   But the prob-

lem is much deeper than that. Rights discourse is internally inconsistent, vacuous or circular. Legal thought can generate equally plausible rights justifications for almost any result. Moreover, the discourse of rights imposes constraints on those who use it that make it almost impossible for it to function effectively as a tool of radical transformation. Rights are by their nature "formal," meaning that they secure to individuals legal protection for as well as from arbitrariness--to speak of rights is precisely <u>not</u> to speak of justice between social classes, races or sexes. Rights discourse, moreover, simply presupposes or takes for granted that the world is and should be divided between a state sector that enforces rights and a private world of "civil society" in which individuals and groups pursue their diverse goals. This framework is, <u>in itself</u>, a part of the problem rather than of the solution. It makes it difficult even to conceptualize radical proposals such as, for example, decentralized democratic worker control of factories.

Because it is logically incoherent and manipulable, traditionally individualist, and willfully blind to the realities of <u>substantive</u> inequality, rights discourse is a trap. As long as one stays within it, one can produce good pieces of argument about the occasional case on the periphery where everyone recognizes value judgments have to be made. But one is without guidance in deciding what to do about fundamental questions, and fated to the gradual loss of confidence in the convincingness of what one has to say in favor of the very results one believes in most passionately.

The alternative left stance is to undertake the Procrustean task of reinterpreting every judicial action as the expression of class interest. One may adopt a conspiracy theory, in which judges deliberately subordinate "justice" (usually just a left-liberal rights theory) to the short run financial interests of the ruling class, or a much more subtle thesis about the "logic" or "needs" or "structural prerequisites" of a particular "stage of monopoly capitalism."

However one sets out to do it, there are two difficulties. The first is that there is just too much drek, too much raw matter of the legal system, and too little time, to give everything you have to study a sinister significance. It would be a full time job just to give instrumental Marxist accounts of the cases on consideration doctrine in first year contracts. Exactly why is it that late nineteenth century capitalism needed to render an uncle's promise to pay his nephew a handsome sum, if he didn't smoke 'til age 21, a legal nullity? Or was it the other way around: that capitalism needed such promises to be underlineable?

The second difficulty is that there is no "logic" to monopoly capitalism, and law cannot be usefully understood, by someone who has to deal with it in all its complexity, as "superstructural." Legal rules the state enforces, and legal concepts that permeate all aspects of social thought, constitute capitalism as well as responding to the interests that operate within it. Law is an aspect of the social totality, not just the tail of the dog. The rules in force are a factor in the power or impotence of all social actors (though they certainly do not determine outcomes in the way liberal legalists sometimes suggest they do).

Because it is part of the equation of power rather than simply a function of it, people struggle for power through law, constrained by their limited understanding and limited ability to predict the consequences of their maneuvers. To understand law is to understand this struggle as an aspect of class struggle <u>and</u> as an aspect of the human struggle to grasp the conditions of social justice. The outcomes of struggle are not preordained by any aspect of the social totality, and the outcomes within law have no "inherent logic" that would allow one to predict outcomes "scientifically," or to reject in advance specific attempts by judges and lawyers to work limited transformations of the system.

Left-liberal rights analysis submerges the student in legal rhetoric, but, because of its inherent vacuousness, can provide no more than an emotional stance against the legal order. The instrumental Marxist approach is highly critical of law, but also dismissive. It is no help in coming to grips with the particularity of rules and rhetoric, because it treats them, a priori, as mere window dressing. In each case, left theory fails left students because it offers no base for the mastery of

26   Legal Education and the

ambivalence. What is needed is to think about law in a way
that will allow one to enter into it, to criticize without utterly
rejecting it, and to manipulate it without self-abandonment to
their system of thinking and doing.

Student Evalution

Law schools teach a small number of useful skills. But
they teach them only obliquely. It would threaten the professional ideology and the academic pretensions of teachers to set
about to make their students as good as they can be at the
relatively simple tasks that they will have to perform in practice. But it would also upset the process by which a hierarchical arrangement analogous to that of law school applicants,
law schools, and law firms is established within a given student body.

To teach the repetitive skills of legal analysis effectively,
one would have to isolate the general procedures that make
them up, and then devise large numbers of factual and doctrinal hypotheticals where students could practice those skills,
knowing what they were doing, and learning in every single
case whether their performance was good or bad. As legal
education now works, on the other hand, students do exercises designed to discover what the "correct solution" to a legal problem might be, those exercises are treated as unrelated
to one another, and students receive no feedback at all except

a grade on a single examination at the end of the course. Students generally experience these grades as almost totally arbitrary--unrelated to how much you worked, how much you liked the subject, how much you thought you understood going into the exam, and what you thought about the class and the teacher.

This is silly, looked at as pedagogy. But it is anything but silly when looked at as ideology. The system generates a rank ordering of students based on grades, and students learn that there is little or nothing they can do to change their place in that ordering, or to change the way the school generates it. Grading as practiced teaches the inevitability and also the justice of hierarchy, a hierarchy that is at once unnecessary and false.

It is unnecessary because it is largely irrelevant to what students will do as lawyers. Most of the process of differentiating students into bad, better and good could simply be dispensed with without the slightest detriment to the quality of legal services. It is false, first, because in so much as it does involve the measuring of the real and useful skills of potential lawyers, the differences between students could be "leveled up" at minimal cost, whereas the actual practice of legal education systematically accentuates differences in real capacities. If law schools invested some of the time and money they now put into socratic classes in developing systematic skills training, and committed themselves to giving constant, detailed feedback on student progress in learning those skills, they could graduate the vast majority of all the law students in the country at the level of technical proficiency now achieved by a small minority in each institution.

Law schools convey their factual message to each student about his or her place in the ranking of students along with the implicit corollary that place is individually earned, and therefore deserved. The system tells you that you learned as much as you were capable of learning, and that if you feel incompetent, or that you could have become better at what you do, it is your own fault. Opposition is sour grapes. Students internalize this message about themselves and about the world, and so prepare themselves for all the hierarchies to follow.

Incapacitation for Alternative Practice

Law schools channel their students into jobs in the hierarchy of the bar according to their own standing in the hierarchy of schools. Students confronted with the choice of what to do after they graduate experience themselves as largely helpless: they have no "real" alternative to taking a job in one of the conventional firms that hires from their school. Partly, faculties generate this sense of student helplessness by propagating myths about the character of the different kinds of practice. They extol the forms that are accessible to their students; they subtly denigrate or express envy about the jobs that will be beyond their students' reach; they dismiss as ethically and socially suspect the jobs their students won't have to take.

As for any form of work outside the established system --for example, legal services for the poor, and neighborhood law practice--they convey to students that, although morally exalted, the work is hopelessly dull and unchallenging, and that the possibilities of reaching a standard of living appropriate to a lawyer are slim or non-existent. These messages are just nonsense--the rationalizations of law teachers who long upward, fear status degradation, and above all hate the idea of risk. Legal services practice, for example, is far more intellectually stimulating and demanding, even with a high case load, than most of what corporate lawyers do. It is also more fun.

Beyond this dimension of professional mythology, law schools act in more concrete ways to guarantee that their students will fit themselves into their appropriate niches in the existing system of practice. First, the actual content of what is taught in a given school will incapacitate students from any other form of practice than that allotted graduates of that institution. This looks superficially like a rational adaptation to the needs of the market, but it is in fact almost entirely un-

necessary.   Law schools teach so little, and that so incompe-
tently, that they cannot, as now constituted, prepare students
for more than one career at the bar.   But the reason for this
is that they embed skills training in mystificatory nonsense,
and devote most of their teaching time to transmitting masses
of ill-digested rules.   A more rational system would emphasize
the way to learn law, rather than rules, and skills rather than
answers.   Student capacities would be more equal as a result,
but students would also be much more flexible in what they
could do in practice.

   A second incapacitating device is the teaching of doctrine
in isolation from practice skills.   Students who have no practice skills tend to exaggerate how difficult it is to acquire
them.   There is a distinct lawyers' mystique of the irrelevance
of the "theoretical" material learned in school, and of the crucial importance of abilities that cannot be known or developed
until one is out in the "real world," "on the firing line" and
"in the trenches."   Students have little alternative to getting
training in this dimension of things after law school.   If you
have any choice in the matter, it will seem impractical to think
about setting up your own law firm, and only a little less impractical to go to a small or political or unconventional firm
rather than to one of those that offers the standard package
of post-graduate education.   Law schools are wholly responsible for this situation.   They could quite easily revamp their
curricula so that any student who wanted it would have a
meaningful choice between independence and servility.

Reproduction of Hierarchy   31

A third form of incapacitation is more subtle. Law school, as an extension of the educational system as a whole, teaches students that they are weak, lazy, incompetent and insecure. And it also teaches them that if they are fortunate, and willing to accept dependency, large institutions will take care of them almost no matter what. The terms of the bargain are relatively clear. The institution will set limited, cognizable tasks, and specify minimum requirements in their performance. The student/associate has no other responsibilities than performance of those tasks. The institution takes care of all the contingencies of life, both within the law (supervision and back up from other firm members; firm resources and prestige to bail you out if you make a mistake) and in private life (firms offer money, but also long term job security and delicious benefits packages aimed to reduce risks of disaster). In exchange, you renounce any claim to control your work setting or the actual content of what you do, and agree to show the appropriate form of deference to those above you and condescension to those below.

By comparison, the alternatives are risky. Law school does not train you to run a small law business, to realistically assess the outcome of a complex process involving many different actors, or to enjoy the feeling of independence and moral integrity that comes of creating your own job to serve your own goals. It tries to persuade you that you are barely competent to perform the much more limited roles it allows you,

and strongly suggests that it is more prudent to kiss the lash
than to strike out on your own.

Chapter Three

Hierarchies of the Legal Profession

Throughout their legal education, students are engaged in
reconceiving themselves and the legal profession.   Partly this
is an affair of knowledge.   Students find out things about the
bar and about themselves that they didn't know before, and
the process has a direction--it is a process of loss, of possibilities foreclosed.   Knowledge of professional life renders irrelevant capacities you have but will not be allowed to use.
Newly discovered incapacities of the self make it impossible to
play roles it was easy to fantasize as a college student.

To begin with, there is the fact that most law jobs, and
almost all the jobs at the top of the hierarchy, consist of providing marginally important services to businesses in their
dealings among themselves and with consumers and stray vic-

34   Legal Education and the

tims. Of the remaining jobs, the great majority involve trying
to get money out of the business community in the form of
compensation for injuries to individuals, or of arranging the
private affairs of middle class or upper class people. The
total number of jobs that directly serve the public interest is
small, and the number of jobs that integrate law and left political action is tiny. The notion that lawyers as a group work
at a profession which is intrinsically involved with justice, or
that lawyers are at least on the front lines of class struggle,
is one of the things that allows left students to resolve their
ambivalence enough to go to law school. But in fact the profession is mainly engaged in greasing the wheels of the economy.

       A second crucial piece of information is that this is partly
drudge work, partly puzzle solving (with the narcotically fascinating and morally vacuous quality of, say, bridge), and
partly a macho battle of wills in which all that counts is winning. Most of this work has no discernible moral spin to it,
let alone a political spin. It is not that it is "evil," it is that
it is socially inconsequential, even when you look at it in
terms of the profession as a whole rather than in terms of individual lawyers. It is fulfilling to help people achieve their
objectives (theirs, not yours), to exercise one's skills, to
make money and be respected. That's it.

Reproduction of Hierarchy   35

As dreams of pursuing careers that would be unambiguously good begin to fade, it becomes important that lawyers
submit to hierarchy in concrete ways, as well as in the more
abstract way of abandoning their hope of integrating their jobs
and their politics. One will drudge, solve puzzles and fight
the battle of wills in a law firm.

Many students have a clear sense of the hierarchical role
of lawyers in society, but little sense of just how stratified is
the bar itself. Getting into law school, or getting into an elite
law school seems to parachute them beyond the land of struggle into a realm of assured superiority. They discover some
of how wrong this is through the admissions process, which
firmly establishes that law schools exist on a scale of rank
which has its ambiguities but is unequivocal in its rejections.
But it is still a shock that what your background is, where
you went to law school, and how well you did seem to make an
enormous difference to where you can get a job, what the
actual content of your job will be, and what you can reason-
ably look forward to in the way of professional advancement
over your whole career.

Law firms are ranked just as law schools are (with the
same ambiguity and the same near finality). The lawyers in
the "top" firms make more money, exercise more power and
have more prestige than lawyers in the next rank, these lawyers lord it over those below them, and so forth to the bottom.

The top firms have top clients, work in the top courts, have top office conditions, do more "challenging" work, and are less subject to all kinds of minor pains and humiliations than those lower down.

This hierarchy is illegitimate (it is neither socially necessary nor in accord with any kind of merit) and it is also sick. Many of the badges of top status are things people should shun rather than embrace, such as isolation from egalitarian contact with people of other social classes than one's own, extreme specialization, having people to treat like slaves, and conspicuous consumption. Many of the attributes of top work that are supposed to make it top are mythical: it is often more mechanical, less creative, less socially valuable and less fun than the work done on the next rung down the ladder. But the hierarchy of firms is a social fact. It must be dealt with, consciously or unconsciously, willingly or unwillingly, by all lawyers. It influences the ambitions, the fears, and the concrete actions of all lawyers. And there is nothing, at least for the moment, that law students can do about its existence.

The hierarchy of firms is based in part on the general class, sexual and racial structure of American society. There are lower middle class, middle class and upper middle class lawyers, and because they congregate in groups mainly according to class criteria, there are lower middle, middle and upper middle class law firms. In some, lawyers wear leisure suits,

in others, three piece worsted suits. In some there are photo-
graphs of lawyers' sailboats on the office walls along with the
diplomas; in others there are reproductions of seascapes
bought by wives to brighten things up. There are regional
accents, but also class accents; fancy colleges and unfancy
colleges. There are few blacks anywhere to be seen. Women
are underrepresented in the top firms; within those firms,
they tend to do legal jobs with relatively low prestige (trusts
and estates rather than litigation). In general, the legal universe just reproduces the society around it: most people live
in homogeneous enclaves within which they rigidly observe the
rituals and guard the prerogatives of their station, while vigorously denying that the concept of station has any relevance
to their lives.

The hierarchy of firms is also in part a professional hierarchy. Lawyers in top firms went to higher ranked law
schools and got better grades than lawyers in the next-to-top,
and so on through gradations to the bottom. Within the bar,
it is possible to distinguish oneself as a technically terrific
lawyer and move up a notch or two, or to be such a bad
lawyer one is disgraced and tumbled a rung or two down.

At first glance, it might appear that there would be a
constant tension between the demands of the two hierarchies,
since there is no reason to believe that professional merit is
distributed other than randomly with regard to class, sex or

38   Legal Education and the

race. But there are practices within the system that work to
minimize or altogether eliminate any such tension. The first is
that the class/sex/race system gets hold of people long before
the professional one, and creates them in such a way that they
will, with some legitimating exceptions, appear to deserve on
professional grounds the position that is in fact based on other
things. Your chances of ending up at a "top" law school are
directly proportional to your status at birth.

Second, people who are able to succeed according to existing professional criteria learn that they must also put themselves through a process of assimilation that has nothing to do
with professionalism. Law schools are finishing schools as well
as trade schools, where everyone learns to act more or less
according to the behavioral criteria of the rung of the profession they hope to enter. There are children of lower middle
class parents at Yale, but the student culture is relentlessly
upper middle class. There are children of working class parents at Boston College, but the student culture mixes only
lower middle and middle class styles. The result of the initial
stacking of the system combined with the norm of upward assimilation is that the class/sex/race hierarchy controls the
professional hierarchy rather than being disrupted by it.

Law firms offer security and training only in exchange
for complicity in various further forms of hierarchy. The first
of these is internal to the firm. There is the generational

hierarchy of lawyers, and the sharp occupational hierarchy that separates the lawyers from the secretaries and the secretaries from messengers and maintenance people. The pecking order conditions all of working life. Young lawyers are no more free to disown their hierarchical superiority to the staff than to cast off deference and dependence on partners. It is almost as bad to treat your secretary like a partner as to do the reverse, and no one smiles on a perverse rejection of the rewards and reassurances (flexible hours and expense accounts, for example) that go along with your particular place in the scheme of things.

A second hierarchy is that of the judicial system, in which judges play the role of tin gods, exacting an extraordinary servility from their court personnel and the lawyers and litigants who appear before them. Judges are free to treat, and often do treat those who come before them with a degree of personal arrogance, a sense of entitlement to arbitrariness, and an insistence on deference that provide an extreme model of everything that is wrong with legal hierarchy.

Lawyers are complicit in this behavior: they expect it, and even enjoy the purity of the experience--the absolute character of the submission demanded, with its suggestion of playing a game which is really and truly for keeps. Beyond that, the judicial system is based on the same extreme specialization of function and differentiation of capacities as the hierarchy of the bar and the internal hierarchy of particular firms. All of this deforms the very idea of justice, rendering it at once impersonal, inaccessible to ordinary human understanding and ordinary human practice, and intensely personal, since everything depends, most of the time, on the crotchets and whims of petty dictators.

The third hierarchy relates lawyers to their clients. It works differently for different firms, according to their rank in the hierarchy of the bar. Top firms deal with the managers of large corporations. They engage with them on the basis of an implicit deal: the lawyers accept, even participate enthusiastically in the self-interested, or immoral, or downright criminal behavior of the client, in return for client acquiescence in the charging of ludicrous fees for work that is mainly elementary or mindless, and vastly swollen by conventions of over-research and over-writing. Within their assigned province, the lawyers behave as though they possessed the knowledge of the Delphic oracle.

At the lower levels of the hierarchy, there are different patterns of domination, mainly involving lawyers making decisions for clients, where the client was perfectly capable of deciding on his own or her own, in ways that make things easy for the lawyer, or profitable, or correspond to the lawyer's own morality or preferences. As in corporate law, the whole thing is based on excluding clients from knowledge they would need to decide on their own, while at the same time

mystifying that knowledge. But in many lawyer/client encounters below the top level, there is also social inequality between
the parties, with the lawyer of higher social class than the client, and this hierarchy reenforces and is reenforced by the
professional one.

The final hierarchy that concerns us is the general social
arrangement in which lawyers are treated--even in a country
with a long tradition of anti-lawyer polemicizing--as among the
elite of the nation. Partly this is simply a reflection of the
fact that many lawyers come from the upper middle class to
start with. But it has some small basis in the usefulness of
lawyers' skills and lawyers' knowledge in the actual operation
of legislative and executive politics, and some small basis in
the real importance and value of the legal profession as an expression both of commitment to truth and to helping people.
On this foundation, lawyers have managed to erect a massive
edifice of social prestige and material over-reward. At each
level of the class system, lawyers are granted a measure of
deference and a measure of power altogether disproportionate
to their objective merit. In their group activities, but also in
their individual social lives, they tend to exploit this deference
and to accentuate it by emphasizing the arcane character of
what they know and do.

*   *   *   *   *   *   *

The legal hierarchies I have been describing have three features in common. First, the people involved in each of them have roles, and the roles require different activities and draw on different capacities. There are partners, associates, secretaries and janitors. There are corporate lawyers, business litigation lawyers, real estate lawyers, small time personal injury lawyers. There are lawyers and mere lay people. Second, if we look at each hierarchy as a joint enterprise within which people produce things, participants playing different roles receive unequal rewards, and exercise unequal degrees of power, both over production decisions and over the organization and style of the workplace. This is most obviously true in the highly organized, oligarchical world of the individual firm, but also true of the bar taken as a unit, and of the hierarchical relations of the profession to its clients and to society at large.

Third, each hierarchy operates within a cultural framework that gives a meaning to the differences in activities and capacities, and to the inequality of power and reward. The meaning is that the whole arrangement is based on the natural differences between people, with respect to talent and energy, that it serves the social function of maximizing the quantity and quality of legal services to society, and that it is therefore just. Hierarchy reflects desert. The parties signify their participation in this universe of shared meanings (whether or not they really believe in it) through deferential or imperious behavior towards others, and by "explaining" what is going on in its terms. "Why do some firms make so much more than others, year after year?" "Well, the best firms can charge higher prices than the less good firms. Since they can charge more, they can hire the best law students, so they make even more money. And so on."

Besides having common features (differentiation of activities and capacities, inequality of power and reward, meritocratic legitimating ideology), the hierarchies are related to one another in a functional way. Internally hierarchical firms are the building blocks of the hierarchy of firms, and it is the bar as a whole that is in a hierarchical relation to society at large. The structure of the parts reproduces the structure of the whole, or vice versa, depending on how you look at it. Individuals are to firms as firms are to the bar as the bar is to society.

* * * * * * *

The above description exaggerates the grimness of life after law school. It's true that socially constructive law jobs are a tiny minority of the total, but their absolute number is large--so large that a geographically mobile student with determination is just about certain to find something to do that's politically progressive--eventually. There are progressive neighborhood lawyers, private civil liberties lawyers in their own elite firms, public interest lawyers, legal services lawyers, lawyers for government regulatory agencies, union and insurgent rank and file labor lawyers, and even progressive law teachers. Each of these modes (there are others) has its rewards and problems. In spite of perennial tensions and rivalries among them, and in spite of the generally conservative political climate, the group as a whole is growing, and growing in morale, sophistication and solidarity as well as in numbers.

It is not important for our purpose here to get the picture just right--no one really knows what's going on anyway. The point is rather that <u>some</u> version of the hierarchical reality of the bar impinges on everything that happens to students from about the middle of the first year through graduation. One cannot grasp the political significance of legal education without understanding that the future is present within every moment of a student's experience.

Students themselves, through their activities after they graduate from law school, reproduce this very world, with amazingly little change from generation to generation. The system is <u>there</u> only because <u>they</u> remake it anew every day. They do <u>this in</u> part because law schools persuade them that it is the best possible system, while at the same time disabling them, individually and collectively, from doing anything effective against it if the ideology doesn't "take."

Chapter Four

The Contribution of Legal Education to the
Hierarchies of the Bar

This chapter describes some of the ways in which legal education contributes to the legal hierarchies I described in the last section. The relationship between legal education and legal hierarchy is complex, and I think it's worth going into in some detail because it offers insight into the issue of how hierarchy works in general. I want to distinguish three different ways in which one can see legal education as a causal factor in the persistence of hierarchy within the bar.

The Analogy Effect

The first of these is the simplest and the weakest--it might be called the analogy effect. Legal education has an internal structure very much like that of the bar. Each law school has its arrangement of professors, assistant professors, students and staff, roughly analogous to the internal arrangement of a law firm. Law schools themselves are ranked, with differences in what they teach, how they teach it, how much power they have in the field of legal education, and what rewards their faculties receive. Within the world of legal education, there is a legitimating ideology which explains and justifies these rankings in terms of natural differences in capacities, social utility and fairness. There are patterns of deference through which people signify their participation in this world of shared meanings, as anyone who has attended a meeting of the Association of American Law Schools can testify.

By the analogy effect I mean simply that legal education "resonates" with or "hangs together" with the hierarchical system of the bar. That one system is organized this way makes it seem more natural that another should be, so long as the first is regarded as in fact legitimate. (Of course, it can work the other way, with the delegitimation of one system having a corrosive effect on those regarded as analogous, heh heh.)

The analogy effect is merely formal. It is independent of the actual functional relationship between the two systems. It operates between legal education and law practice, but also between the legal profession and the medical profession, the media, architecture, business management, and even the organization of the shop floor in manufacturing. Because hier-

archy in all these areas is present, looks vaguely similar, relies on the same general meritocratic legitimating ideology, it is
strengthened simply by numbers--it looks like it's "the way
things are."

Legal Ideology as an "Input"

A second way in which legal education relates to legal hierarchy after law school arises from its specialized character
as education.   Law teachers are constantly involved in explaining how the world works, and also in formulating notions
of how it should work.   As it presently operates, legal education is like education in general in that it propagates the message that things are the way they are because it is best, or
close to best that they should be that way.   In other words,
the legal education system produces ideology.   Ideology is one
of its "inputs" into the rest of the social system.   Since the
bar is part of the social system, it benefits from this legitimating contribution.

I am not here speaking of anything law schools teach
about law practice, but about their general message about the
legal rules in force.   Law schools, as we saw above, do more
than teach these rules.   They also teach why they are a good
thing, and that they are there because they are a good thing.
These rules provide the framework within which social actors

create all the hierarchies of our society, including the hierarchies of the bar. If the rules were different--for example, if all bosses were legally obligated to spend part of every day on their own typing, or if secretaries had a legal right to education for upward job mobility--the hierarchies would be different too. In so much as legal education legitimates the rules in force, it legitimates the consequences, in terms of the division of labor and inequality of power and reward, that flow from the rules. By teaching law students that the rules are groovy, law teachers also teach them that they are entitled to the six figure salaries they will earn in corporate law practice, just as doctors and business managers are entitled to theirs.

Within its general ideological message, legal education has some particular things to say to lawyers--namely, that what they do is more than just a craft, like, say carpentry. What they do is "legal reasoning." Law schools are largely (though not exclusively) responsible for persuading lawyers and the lay public that lawyers do more than exercise the skills I described in the section on the curriculum. So they are also at least partly responsible for the hierarchical relations that lawyers manage to erect on that shadowy foundation. The mystique of legal reasoning reenforces all these hierarchies because it makes it seem that people who have gone to law school are privy to secrets that are loaded with social value.

Reproduction of Hierarchy   49

The actual capacities of lawyers--knowledge of rule systems, of issue spotting, case analysis and pro/con policy argu-
ment--have real social value; they are difficult to acquire; and
one can't practice law effectively without them. But they are
nowhere near as inaccessible as they are made to seem by the
mystique of legal education. By mystifying them, law schools
make it seem necessary to restrict them to a small group, pre-
sumed to be super-talented. That, in turn, makes it seem
necessary to divide the labor in the joint enterprise of providing legal services so that most of the participants (secretaries,
paralegals, office assistants, court clerks, janitors, marshalls,
and so on) are firmly and permanently excluded from doing the
things that are most challenging and rewarding within the overall activity. Once they have devalued everyone else on "professional" grounds, it also seems natural for those who have
gone to law school to specialize in the most desirable tasks,
while controlling the whole show and reaping the lion's share
of the rewards.

The Hierarchical Structuring of the Group of Prospective
Lawyers

The third way in which legal education contributes causally to the hierarchies of the bar is by structuring the population of potential lawyers so that it will seem natural, efficient
and fair that they should incorporate themselves into the existing hierarchy of law firms without much changing it. To

grasp this, imagine that by some bizarre chance all the lawyers in the country decided to create a bar of roughly equal firms, in place of the existing hierarchy. Such a program would have many things in its way, even supposing the decision to pursue it was unanimous, including the influence by analogy of all the other hierarchies of our society, and the ideological messages about existing legal arrangements, and about the nature of legal reasoning, that the schools now propagate.

But the program of equalization would also have to contend with the fact that law school graduates enter practice as a group already structured hierarchically. They already have different capacities, different values and expectations, and different visions of what law practice should be. There is more to it than difference: they are unequal, in many though by no means all respects, before they have even begun.

The internal structure of the group corresponds roughly to the structure of the bar: some prospective lawyers are prepared for elite practice, others for small time solo practice. The whole group tends most of the time to believe that these differences among themselves, these inequalities, flow from individual characteristics, from their personal virtues and vices, talents and energies.

Reproduction of Hierarchy   51

Against this background, it seems an almost inescapable inference that <u>these</u> prospective lawyers should be organized into a hierarchy of firms that will reflect and exploit for social good the differences among them. The group itself is likely to see this as a desirable or at least as a fair outcome, one that gives people what they deserve. Yet this seeming inevitability is in large part, though of course not entirely, a product of the way the collectivity of law teachers has chosen to organize its joint enterprise of legal education.

The teachers' fundamental structuring practice is the creation and maintenance of a hierarchy of law schools. This involves at least three subpractices: First, law teachers create an ordering of schools according to material resources and faculty academic qualifications (the richest schools tend as a general matter to have the most academically qualified faculty rather than the least qualified). Second, law teachers arrange law school applicants in an ordering according to "corrected" college grades and LSAT scores. Third, law teachers allocate students to schools so that the "better" students go to the "better" schools.

The upshot is a system in which some schools have lots of money, "good" teachers, and "good" students. Other schools have middling money, teachers and students. The bottom schools have little money, "bad" teachers and "bad" students. (Of course, some schools defy such easy characterization, but not many.)

There is nothing "natural" about this situation. Indeed, there are several European countries in which all the law schools are more or less equal (though by no means identical one to another) in terms of money, students and faculty. Law teachers in this country could set out to equalize the schools and then do what was necessary to keep them equal. For example, we could assign teachers to schools at random (perhaps with a regional preference), equalize per student expenditures, and assign the "worst" students to the schools that looked "best" educationally. We could periodically scramble faculty and facilities in order to prevent temporary advantages from ripening into permanent hierarchy. The schools could be kept small enough so that random student and teacher assignment would produce a flowering of real differences rather than the current lockstep.

The pool of prospective lawyers would look very different if law teachers chose to form it in this way. Legal education would facilitate rather than obstruct efforts to democratize the bar. What would be lost?

In so far as the hierarchy of schools works on its own terms--that is, makes sure that the most promising students get the most material resources, the best teachers and the most advanced academic program--it needs some justification because it intentionally accentuates inequality. I don't think it's remotely possible to justify the inequality on the ground that the total pool of prospective lawyers is more socially valuable if educated in this skewed way than it would be if all law students had equal access to educational resources. Indeed, with some affirmative redistribution of resources and a lot of conscious effort we could level entering students up, so as to sharply reduce the inequality of educational outcome while raising the average level, and not lowering the abilities of those at the top. I think we'd deliver better legal services to more people as a result. The hierarchy of schools is unnecessary as well as unfair.

It's just a confusion to think that an egalitarian system would involve more (or less) compulsion than what we have now. Today, the compulsion is in the form of testing and certification, followed by forced allocation of students and faculty to institutions according to their rank ordering. Choice is within a particular level. An egalitarian system would exercise compulsion through a cut-off: some kind of testing and certification of minimum competence to be a teacher or a student. The cut-off would be the subject of struggle. However the struggle came out, it would represent the forced exclusion of many aspirants to legal careers. But once the cut-off occurred, an egalitarian system based substantially on chance could offer students and faculty a lot more choice among equal (but by no means identical) institutions than they now enjoy. The existing system is no more "free" than it is natural or efficient.

It would, however, be much worse--perhaps intolerable--if it worked better on its own terms. As things now stand, it is only "better" students in quotation marks that get allocated to schools that are themselves only "better" in quotation marks. Law school criteria for hiring and promoting faculty are so arbitrary with respect to any intelligible notion of merit that they partially randomize faculty composition (though the criteria are anything but random with respect to race, sex and class). The student admission index has the same effect, scattering good students across the whole spectrum of schools. The system as a whole is so arbitrary and so plainly corrupted by class, racial and sexual bias that people at the "lower" levels have no reason to see themselves as inferior, in spite of the heavy meritocratic ideology and the amazing smugness of the supposed elite.

No one aspect of legal education is crucial to the process by which law teachers structure the group of prospective lawyers. For example, law teachers could make a real effort to equalize law schools and then keep them equal, but still rank students in an admissions process, compete for the "best" among them, narrow them through specialized curricula, and grade them. Or suppose that law school admission was by random selection from the pool that could meet a set of minimum requirements for socially constructive law practice. It would still be possible to have a hierarchy of schools.

Reproduction of Hierarchy   55

It is nonetheless the case that all the practices point in the same direction, and reenforce one another. The inequality among students that is asserted when schools rank applicants gets accentuated when they choose to give the less promising a worse education than the more promising, and when they choose to educate them in ways that cut off their access to the capacities that are valued in the "top" schools. The system of student evaluation intensifies the structuring effect of admissions, school hierarchy and curriculum through the message that grades are somehow objective (though you experience them as arbitrary) so that it is hopeless to try to improve your performance, more than marginally, after the first year.

The Role of Physical Violence in the Structuring Process

There is a real element of force--of physical violence--in the structuring process, though it is easy to lose sight of it, so completely do the participants internalize its norms. If you try to go to Harvard in spite of having gotten in only to Suffolk, the school will eventually call the police and have you taken off the premises, violently taken if you resist. They will believe that you are crazy, rather than criminal, as it seems unlikely that any sane person would challenge the system in this way, so you probably won't go to jail.

Or suppose you were to join together with other students to   demand   that all law schools   share their resources on the basis of an equal number of dollars expended per student. You could talk all you wanted, but if you all sat in in your classrooms, there would come a moment when the administration would appeal to the rule of law, meaning in this case the rule that what they say goes, and threaten, at least, to call for as many policemen as were necessary to force you out. That this almost never happens does not make it one whit less real an influence on the behavior of everyone involved, especially since everyone seems to me to overestimate the actual willingness and ability of those in formal, legal control to play hardball rather than negotiate.

But if it were only a matter of force, our imagined collectivity of lawyers trying to equalize law firms would treat the structuring activities of law teachers as a relatively unimportant obstacle. What makes things much worse than that is that law teachers as a group successfully persuade most law students that in truth the best students have been fitted to the best schools, that the best schools are in fact better and teach better things, and that the better students at any given school are rewarded with better grades. Law teachers indoctrinate students to believe that people and institutions arrange themselves naturally in hierarchies, and that the hierarchy they have been involved with for three years is a particularly legitimate because particularly meritocratic one.

Reproduction of Hierarchy   57

   To protest against this system seems like sour grapes--
morally unsavory as well as practically futile. To change it,
say by applying the legal rules about racial and sexual discrimination that are a matter of course for blue collar jobs (under
the Supreme Court's <u>Griggs</u> decision requiring objective validation of job qualification tests that have a disproportionate impact on minorities) seems to risk serious social malfunction,
and serious injustice to individuals entitled to just rewards for
"their" talents.

Chapter Five

The Modeling of Hierarchical Relationships

Yet another way in which legal education contributes causally to the hierarchies of the bar is through the practices of law teachers that model for students how they are supposed to think, feel and act in their future professional roles. Some of this is a matter of teaching by example, some of it a matter of more active learning from interactions that are a kind of clinical education for lawyerlike behavior.

This training is a major factor in the hierarchical life of the bar. It encodes the message of the legitimacy of the whole system into the smallest details of personal style, daily routine, gesture, tone of voice, facial expression, a plethora of little p's and q's for everyone to mind. Partly these will serve as a language--a way for the young lawyer to convey that she knows what the rules of the game are, and intends to play by them. Partly, it is a matter of ritual oaths and affirmations--by adopting the mannerisms one pledges one's troth to inequality. And partly it is a substantive matter of value. Hierarchical behavior will come to express and realize the hierarchical selves of people who were initially only wearers of masks.

A first lesson is that professors are intensely preoccupied with the status rankings of their schools, and show themselves willing to sacrifice to improve their status in the rankings, and to prevent downward drift. They approach the appointment of colleagues in the spirit of trying to get people who are as high up as possible in a conventionally defined hierarchy of teaching applicants, and they are notoriously hostile to affirmative action in faculty hiring, even when they are quite willing to practice it for student admissions and in filling administrative posts. Assistant professors begin their careers as the little darlings of their older colleagues. They end up in tense competition for the prize of tenure, trying to accommodate themselves to standards and expectations that are, typically, too vague to master except by a commitment to please at any cost. In these respects, law schools are a good preview of what law firms will be like.

Law professors, like lawyers, have secretaries. Students deal with them off and on through law school, watch how their bosses treat them, how they treat their bosses, and how "a secretary" relates to "a professor" even when one does not work for the other. Students learn that it is acceptable, even if it's not always and everywhere the norm, for faculty to treat their secretaries petulantly, condescendingly, with a perfectionism that is a matter of the boss' face rather than of the demands of the job itself, as though they were personal body servants, utterly impersonally, or as objects of sexual harassment.

They learn that "a secretary" treats "a professor" with elaborate deference, as though her time and her dignity meant nothing and his everything, even when he is not her boss. In general, they learn that humane relations in the workplace are a matter of the superior's grace, rather than of human need and social justice.

These lessons are repeated in the relationships of professors and secretaries with administrators and with maintenance and support staff. Teachers convey a sense of their own superiority, and practice a social segregation sufficiently extreme so that there are no occasions on which the reality of that superiority might be tested. As a group, they accept the division of labor that consigns everyone in the institution but them to boredom and stagnation. Friendly but deferential social relations reenforce everyone's sense that all's for the best, making hierarchy seem to disappear in the midst of cordiality, when in fact any serious challenge to the regime would be met with outrage and retaliation.

All of this is teaching by example. In their relations with students, and in the student culture they foster, teachers get the message across more directly and more powerfully. The student/teacher relationship is the model for relations between junior associates and senior partners, and also for the relationship between lawyers and judges. The student/student relationship is the model for relations among lawyers as peers, for the age cohort within a law firm, and for the "fraternity" of the courthouse crowd.

In the classroom and out of it, students learn a particular style of deference. They learn to suffer with positive cheerfulness interruption in mid-sentence, mockery, ad hominem assault, inconsequent asides, questions that are so vague as to be unanswerable but can somehow be answered wrong all the same, abrupt dismissal, and stinginess of praise (even if these things are not always and everywhere the norm).

They learn, if they have talent, that submission is most effective flavored with a pinch of rebellion, to bridle a little before they bend. They learn to savor crumbs, while picking from the air the indications of the master's mood that can mean the difference between a good day and misery. They learn to take it all in good sort, that his Clark is worse than his Byse, that there is often shyness, good intentions, some real commitment to your learning something behind the authoritarian facade. So it will be with many a robed curmudgeon in years to come.

Then there is affiliation. From among many possibilities, each student gets to choose a mentor, or several, to admire and depend on, to become sort of friends with if the mentor is a liberal, to sit at the feet of if the mentor is more "traditional." You learn how he or she is different from other teachers, and to be supportive of those differences, as the mentor learns something of your particular strengths and weaknesses, both of you trying to prevent the inevitability of letters of recommendation from corrupting the whole experience. This can be fruitful and satisfying, or degrading, or both at once. So it will be a few years later with your "father in the law."

There is another, more subtle, less conscious message conveyed in student/teacher relations. Teachers are overwhelmingly white, male and middle class, and most (by no means all) black and women law teachers give the impression of thorough assimilation to that style, or of insecurity and unhappiness. Students who are women or black or working class find out something important about the professional universe from the first day of class: that it is only nominally pluralist in cultural terms. The teacher sets the tone--a white, male, middle class tone. Students adapt. They do so partly out of fear, partly out of hope of gain, partly out of genuine admiration for their role models.   But the line between adaptation to the intellectual and skills content of legal education and adaptation to the white, male, middle class cultural style is a fine one, easily lost sight of.

While students quickly understand that there is diversity among their fellow students and that the faculty is not really homogeneous in terms of character, background or opinions, the classroom itself becomes more rather than less uniform as legal education progresses.   You'll find Fred Astaire and Howard Cosell, over and over again, but never Richard Pryor or Betty Friedan.   It's not that the teacher punishes you if you use slang or wear clothes or give examples or voice opinions that identify you as different, though that <u>might</u> happen. You are likely to be sanctioned, mildly or severely, only if you refuse to adopt the highly cognitive, dominating mode of discourse that everyone identifies as lawyerlike.   Nonetheless, the indirect pressure for conformity is intense.

If alone in your seat you feel alienated in this atmosphere, it is unlikely that you will do anything about it in the classroom setting itself, however much you gripe about it with friends.   It is more than likely that you'll find a way, in class, to respond as the teacher seems to want you to respond--to be a lot like him, as far as one could tell if one knew you only in class, even though your imitation is flawed by the need to suppress anger.

And when some teacher, at least once in some class, makes a remark that seems sexist or racist, or seems unwilling to treat black or women students in quite as "challenging" a way as white students, or treats them in a more challenging way, or cuts off discussion when a woman student gets mad at a male student's joke about the tort of "offensive touching," it is unlikely that you'll do anything then either.

It is easy enough to see this situation of enforced cultural uniformity as oppressive, but somewhat more difficult to see it as training, especially if you are aware of it and hate it. But it is training nonetheless. You will pick up mannerisms, ways of speaking, gestures, which would be "neutral" if they were not emblematic of membership in the white middle class male universe of the bar. You will come to expect to live as a lawyer in a world in which essential parts of you are not represented, or are misrepresented, and in which things you don't like are accepted to the point that it doesn't occur to people that they are even controversial. And you will come to expect that there is nothing you can do about it.

One develops ways of coping with these expectations-- turning off attention or involvement when the conversation strays in certain directions, participating actively while ignoring the offensive elements of the interchange, even re-interpreting as inoffensive things that would otherwise make you boil. These are skills that incapacitate rather than empower, skills that will help you imprison yourself in practice.

Relations among students get a lot of their color from relations with the faculty.   There is the sense of blood brother-
hood, with or without sisters, in endless speculation about the
Olympians.   The speculation is colored with rage, expressed
sometimes in student theatricals, or the "humor" column of the
school paper.   ("Put Professor X's talents to the best possible
use: Turn him into hamburger."   Ha, ha.)   There is likely to
be a surface norm of non-competitiveness and cooperation.
("Gee, I thought this would be like The Paper Chase.")   But
a basic thing to learn is the limits of that cooperation.   Very
few people can combine rivalry for grades, good summer jobs,
clerkships, with helping another member of the study group
so effectively that he might actually pose a danger.   You learn
camaraderie and distrust at the same time.   So it will be in the
law firm age cohort.

Often, it boils down to law review.   At first, everyone
claims they aren't interested, wouldn't want to put in the time,
don't work hard enough to make it, can't stand the elitism of
the whole thing.   But most students give about equal time to
fantasies of flunking out and fantasies of grabbing the brass
ring.   And even though the class has been together for a
semester or a year, everything is still different after the
lightning of grades.   An instant converts jerks into statesmen;
honored spokespeople retire to the margins, shamed.   Try proposing that law review should be open to anyone who will do
the work.   Within a week or two, the new members have a

66   Legal Education and the

dozen arguments for competitive selection. Likewise at the hour of partnership.

There is more to it than that. Through the reactions of fellow students--diffuse, disembodied events that just "happen," in class or out of class--women learn how important it is not to appear to be "hysterical females," and that when your wimpy, hopeful moot court partner gets a crush on you, and doesn't know it, and is married, there is a danger he will hate you when he discovers what he has been feeling. Lower middle class students learn not to wear an undershirt that shows, and that certain patterns and fabrics in clothes will stigmatize them no matter what their grades.

Black students learn without surprise that the bar will have its own peculiar forms of racism, and that their very presence means affirmative action, unless it means "he would have made it even without affirmative action." They wonder about forms of bias so diabolical even they can't see them, and whether legal reasoning is intrinsically white. Meanwhile, dozens of small changes through which they become more and more like other middle or upper middle class Americans engender rhetoric about how the black community is not divided along class lines. On one level, all of this is about how to make partner. But on another, it's just high school replayed.

Reproduction of Hierarchy   67

   The senior prom is the annual dinner of a student honor
society (the law review, the moot court organization). The
atmosphere is dreamlike: people are the same but dressed differently, nervously "seated" with faculty scattered among the
tables, so that each group will be a little microcosm of the
grown-up world to come. Husbands of law students aren't
there, or if they are, they tend to shut up and think of other
things. But for the student and wife couple, the occasion is
likely to dangerously charged.

   A wife is a professional asset, but not all wives are of
equal value. A wife who came with you from where you came
from may have hung back in your student apartment for three
years, not liking your new friends, learning no new ways.
She may embarrass you in front of a teacher (partner) or just
fail to fit into the convivial chatter. Or maybe she sallied
forth, and doesn't see herself first and foremost as an asset.
Maybe she's waiting to pounce the minute you show your
phony career colors.

   This is a rehearsal. It's time for the two of you to
strike some kind of deal that will see you through a dozen or
a hundred social functions in the years to come. Often, the
deal seems to extend the demands of hierarchy--for deference,
for falseness--from the workplace into the home. Your wife
learns to fit herself into the periphery of acquaintances around
the animated core of shoptalkers, maybe finding someone with

whom to conspire, maybe only endless bland chatter. Her demeanor, ideally, acknowledges that this is your show not hers, that the rule is, "above all do your husband no harm," not even by showing you're bored or offended, let alone by disrupting the smooth conventional flow. We (partners) expect you to deliver her performance, just as we might expect you to deliver a memo. The two of you may find a way to evade or challenge this arrangement. If not, you'll owe her for her submission, though it be offered at first as a gift, or with no sense of imposition on her part.

And what about the pretty, aggressive, anti-feminist law student who has spent more hours with the student-husband over the last year than his wife, and is controlling the professor (partner) with her subtle combination of flirtatious hostess and hip mentee? As of now, she seems to have everyone on the run or running after her. But she may also hate herself for it, and none of us knows how her lonely strategy will stand a test of years.

The culmination of law school as training for professional hierarchy is the placement process, with the form of the culmination depending on where your *school fits in the pecking order.* At the bottom, placement says it all by its absence: there's a bulletin board on which local government agencies indicate their willingness to receive applications, and everyone knows the way you get a job is by hustling one. Failing that, you just hang out your shingle, hoping a legal education designed for something else entirely doesn't get you in such bad trouble you're disbarred.

Toward the middle of the ranking, firms show up on campus to display their relative status within the bar, and the bar as a whole affirms its hierarchical values and the rewards they bring. At the top are the students who go through the elaborate procedures of the big firms, including, nowadays, first year summer jobs, dozens of interviews, fly-outs, second year summer jobs, more interviews, and more fly-outs.

This system allows law firms to get a social sense of applicants, a sense of how they will contribute to the non-legal image of the firm and to the internal system of deference and affiliation. It allows the big firms to convey to students the extraordinary opulence of the life they offer, adding the allure of free travel, expense account meals, fancy hotel suites and parties at country clubs to the simple message of big bucks in a paycheck. And it teaches students at "fancy" law schools, students who have had continuous experience of academic and careerist success, that they are not as "safe" as they thought they were.

When students at Columbia or Yale paper dorm corridors with rejection letters, or award prizes for the most rejection letters and for the most unpleasant single letter, they show

their sense of the meaning of the ritual. There are many
ways in which the boss can persuade you to brush his teeth
and comb his hair. One of them is to arrange things so that
almost all students get good jobs, but most students get their
good job through twenty interviews yielding only two offers.

By dangling the bait, making clear the rules of the game,
and then subjecting almost everyone to intense anxiety about
their acceptability, firms structure entry into the profession so
as to maximize acceptance of hierarchy. If you feel you've succeeded, you're forever grateful, and you have a vested interest. If you feel you've failed, you blame yourself, when you
aren't busy feeling envy. When you get to be the hiring partner, you'll have a visceral understanding of what's at stake,
but it will be hard even to imagine why someone might want to
change it.

Insomuch as these hierarchies are generational, they are
easier to take than those baldly reflective of race, sex or
class. You, too, will one day be a senior partner and, who
knows, maybe even a judge; you will have mentees, and be
the object of the rage and longing of those coming up behind
you. Training for subservience is training for domination as
well. Nothing could be more natural, and, if you've served
your time, more fair, than that you as a group should do as
you have been done to, for better and for worse. But it

doesn't <u>have</u> to be that way, and remember, you saw it first in law school.

$$* \quad * \quad * \quad * \quad * \quad * \quad *$$

I have been arguing that legal education causes legal hierarchy. Legal education supports it by analogy, provides it a general legitimating ideology by justifying the rules that underlie it, and provides it a particular ideology by mystifying legal reasoning. Legal education structures the pool of prospective lawyers so that their hierarchical organization seems inevitable, and trains them in detail to look and think and act just like all the other lawyers in the system.

Up to now, I have presented this causal analysis as though legal education were a machine feeding particular inputs into another machine. But machines have no consciousness of one another; insomuch as they are coordinated, it is by some external intelligence. Law teachers, on the other hand, have a vivid sense of what the profession looks like, and of what it expects them to do. Actors in the two systems consciously adjust to one another, and also consciously attempt to influence one another. (Legal education is a product of legal hierarchy as well as a cause of it.)

To my mind, this means that law teachers must take responsibility for legal hierarchy in general, not just for hier-

archy within legal education. If it is there, it is there because they put it there, and reproduce it generation after generation, just as lawyers do.

Chapter Six

The Student Response to Hierarchy

Students respond in different ways to their slowly emerging consciousness of the hierarchical realities of life in the law.   Looking around me, I see students who enter wholeheartedly into the system--for whom the training "takes" in a quite straightforward way.   Others appear, at least, to manage something more complex.   They accept the system's presentation of itself as largely neutral, as apolitical, meritocratic, instrumental, a matter of craft.   And they also accept the system's promise that if they do their work, "serve their time" and "put in their hours," they are free to think and do and feel anything they want in their "private lives."

This mode of response is complex, because the message, though sincerely proffered, is not truly meant.   People who accept the message at face value often seem to sense that what has actually transpired is different.   And since the law is neither apolitical nor meritocratic nor instrumental nor a matter of craft (at least not exclusively these things), and since training for hierarchy cannot be a matter merely of public as opposed to private life, it is inevitable that they do in fact give and take something different than what is suggested by the overt terms of the bargain.

Sometimes people enact a kind of parody: they behave in a particularly tough, cognitive, lawyer-like mode in their professional lives, and construct a private self that seems on the surface to deliberately exaggerate opposing qualities of warmth, sensitivity, easygoingness or cultural radicalism. Sometimes one senses an opposite version: the person never fully enters into "legal reasoning," remaining always a slightly disoriented, not-quite-in-good-faith role-player in professional life, and feels a parallel inability ever to fully "be" his private self.   For example, he may talk "shop" and obsess about the day at work, while hating himself for being unable to "relax," but then find that at work he is unable to make the tasks assigned him fully his own, and that each new task seems at first an unpleasant threat to his fragile feelings of confidence.

For left students there is another possibility, which might be called the denunciatory mode.   One can take law school work seriously as time-serving, and do it coldly in that spirit, hate one's fellow students for their surrenders, and focus one's hopes on "not being a lawyer," or on a fantasy of an unproblematically leftist legal job on graduation. This response is hard from the very beginning. If you reject what teachers and the student culture tell you about what the first year curriculum means and how to enter into learning it, you are adrift as to how to go about becoming minimally competent. You have to develop a theory on your own of what is valid skills training and what merely indoctrination, and your ambivalent desire to be successful in spite of all is likely to sabotage your independence. As graduation approaches, it becomes clearer that there are precious few unambiguously virtuous law jobs even to apply for, and your situation begins to look more like everyone else's, though perhaps more extreme. Most (by no means all) students who begin with denunciation end by settling for some version of the bargain of public against private life.

I am a good deal more confident about the patterns that I have just described than about the attitudes toward hierarchy that go along with them. My own position in the system of class, sex and race (as an upper middle class white male), and my rank in the professional hierarchy (as a Harvard professor) give me an interest in the perception that hierarchy is both omnipresent and enormously important, even while I am busy condemning it. And there is a problem of imagination that goes beyond that of interest. It is hard for me to know whether I even understand the attitudes toward hierarchy of women and blacks, for example, or of children of working class parents, or of solo practitioners eking out a living from residential real estate closings.

Members of those groups sometimes suggest that the par-ticularity of their experience of oppression cannot be grasped by outsiders, but sometimes that the failure to grasp it is per-sonal rather than inevitable. It sometimes seems to me that all people have at least analogous experiences of the oppressive reality of hierarchy, even those who seem most favored by the system--that the collar feels the same when you get to the end of the rope, whether the rope is ten feet long or fifty.   On the other hand, it seems clear that hierarchy creates distances that are never bridged.

It is not uncommon for a person to answer a description of the hierarchy of law firms like the one I gave above with a flat denial that the bar is really ranked. Lawyers of lower middle class background tend to have far more direct political power in the state governments than "elite" lawyers, even under Republican administrations. Furthermore, every lawyer knows of instances of real friendship outside and beyond the distinctions that are supposed to be so important, and can cite examples of lower middle class lawyers in upper middle class law firms, and vice versa. There are many lawyers who seem to defy hierarchical classification, and law firms and law

schools that do likewise, so that one can argue that the claim
that everyone and everything is ranked breaks down the minute you try to give concrete examples. I have been told often
enough that I may be right about the pervasiveness of ranking, but that the speaker has never noticed it himself, himself
treats all lawyers in the same way, regardless of their class or
professional standing, and has never, except in an occasional
very bizarre case, found lawyers violating the egalitarian
norm.

When the person making these claims is a rich corporate
lawyer who was my prep school classmate, I tend to interpret
them as a willful denial of the way he is treated and treats
others. When the person speaking is someone I perceive as
less favored by the system (say, a woman of lower middle
class origin who went to Brooklyn Law School and now works
for a small struggling downtown law firm), it is harder to
know how to react. Maybe I'm just wrong about what it's like
out there. Maybe my preoccupation with the horrors of hierarchy is just a way to wring the last ironic drop of pleasure
from my own hierarchical superiority. But I don't interpret it
that way. The denial of hierarchy is false consciousness.
The problem is not whether hierarchy is there, but how to understand it, and what its implications are for political action.

Chapter Seven

The Politics of Hierarchy

There are at least three different reasons for being against legal hierarchy in the form I have just described. Taking it on its own meritocratic terms, the game is stacked in favor of white males of the middle and upper middle class, so that power and reward are not distributed according to merit as merit would be revealed in a system of equal opportunity. Again, taking the system on its own terms, it is socially irrational: it is not necessary to have as many differences of capacity and role or as much inequality of power and reward as we now have, in order to achieve our social purposes.

I subscribe to both of these criticisms, but I don't think they go nearly far enough, since in each case they treat legal hierarchy as <u>in itself</u> socially neutral. Even if the rank orderings of law school applicants, law schools, law students, and law firms were accurately reflective of merit and optimally adjusted to achieving the benefits of the division of labor, I would be against them. The attitudes, behaviors and relationships associated with legal hierarchy constitute, in themselves, a social perversion.

To the very limited extent that legal hierarchy flows from the division of labor and from differences in individual talent (whether we think these have an irreducible genetic base or are merely the inescapable consequence of the socialization of children), it <u>may</u> be a necessary evil. But it is something to be hated even as we enjoy its benefits, and it is an argument against living in a way that requires those benefits.

As a matter of fact, I don't think we'd lose anything at all in terms of social product if lawyers, law professors, secretaries, paralegals and law firm janitors were all paid exactly the same amount. I don't think we'd lose anything if we abolished the hierarchy of law schools by equalizing dollars per student and assigning professors to schools at random. Or if we attacked the division of labor and the differentiation of capacities in law firms through training and rotation for everyone through all law jobs. We could and should go further: we should attack the spirit of hierarchy as it manifests itself in ideology and in all the details of expressive behavior discussed in the last chapter.

These judgments are not logical implications of some more general social or political theory. I believe that legal hierarchy is an evil and unnecessary on the basis of my own and my friends' lived experience within it. Both the ethical and the factual judgments involved are specific, grounded in late night conversations, flashes of insight, rebellious moments, and moments of failure, of self-betrayal and betrayal of others (dear ones). All of this takes place in a context of interest, even immersion, in theory. But I have no intention of proposing a New Analysis, based on a New Concept (reproduction of hierarchy), that might replace traditional thinking in terms, say, of race, sex or class.

What I like about the word hierarchy is its vagueness, which makes it useless for purposes of "real," hard-edged theory. To use it is to deny that class, or gender, or, say, the relation of imperialist countries to Third World peoples, is the fundamental category. It's even vaguer than that: it includes forms of meritocratic and generational hierarchy within organizations that could sustain themselves even without the economic and cultural structures of class, race and sex. It's the whole banana we're against, not just one or another slice of it.

Vagueness has its price. The notion of hierarchy encompasses lots of relationships that don't seem to me perverse, and others that seem ambiguous. The notion itself doesn't tell

Reproduction of Hierarchy   81

us which hierarchies are ok and which are awful. For example, I think parents should have some authority over children, that students sometimes legitimately revere teachers, and
that children should sometimes coercively care for their aged
parents.   Sometimes the only response to what one sees as
false consciousness is to take responsibility for "forcing people
to be free," and it is self-delusive to pretend that one can do
this without an element of structured inequality creeping into
the relationship.

Hierarchy isn't even an inclusive term to describe the
evils of our system. There would be lots wrong (for example,
our relation to the environment) even if we cleaned up our unequal structures. And there are other evils (sexual jealousy)
that may be ineradicable.

What makes one a radical, in this view, is not that one is
against hierarchy, since we all sometimes accept it, nor that
one is against "illegitimate" hierarchy, since we're all against
that. Nor is the radical the person with the theory that "goes
to the root." None of us has such a theory. The radical is
the person who wants to go further, right now, practically, to
dismantle existing structures of hierarchy that look evil, and
wants to go further, right now, practically, in confronting or
subverting the forces that keep them in place.

82   Legal Education and the

It's a relational concept.   There are no absolute radicals, just people being radical in particular situations.   People don't (at least in my experience) get to be like that by deduction from general principles.   There's no more reason to hope you can convert them by logic than to fear they'll desert if the theory isn't right.   It's more like you wake up one morning knowing that you aren't going to stand some abuse or injustice for another day, not knowing what will happen as a result, not even sure you can justify whatever it is you're about to do.

Sometimes things bubble to the surface in a group of friends that sound more oppositional than you thought you were, and they support rather than shun you.   Or an opponent treats what you thought was a moderate statement as advocacy of "socialism" or "radical feminism," and you find yourself defiantly embracing the label instead of weasling out of it.   It's then one begins to want theory--to want it as a way to express one's new orientation, rather than to determine its content or serve it as an instrument.

But if theory is expressive, rather than determinative of the content of political struggle, what check is there against error?   Against passivity--the influenza of groups dispersed in the chambers of the belly of the monster?   Against murderous totalitarian self-righteousness should we ever have the power to do anyone real harm?   If a check means a rational mechanism to confirm that one has not fallen into error, there is none. The only check against internal murderousness and passivity is the criticism of friends. The only check against the murderousness and passivity of friends is opposition to them. The will to leave them if necessary.

It might seem to follow from this chastened view of the role of theory that we can talk only about the small slice of the world about which we can be truly knowledgeable. As we generalize, we float free of our experiential ground, and our theorizing loses its only possible validation.

Yet we live in the great world as well as in the little. We belong to groups that extend beyond particular places and we speak a language--the conceptual, scientific, social theoretical, aesthetic-modernist language of the world bourgeoisie--that aspires to universality. If it is to perform its expressive function, our theory must help us grasp this transcendent aspect of our experience, as well as our dispersal in corners and cul de sacs.

It's not a question of grasping an essence of our total situation from which we could reason to particular proposals. It's more the projection onto the widest screen of the ideas and images that develop in the course of small-scale, backwater actions that we long to join into the great stream. What follows is an attempt at that kind of general theory from an

84   Legal Education and the

existential-Marxist, anarcho-syndicalist, modernist point of view (recognizing that such a conjunction of labels doesn't tell much).

It is also an attempt to reconstruct the world from the particular perspective of the radical law student or law teacher whose dilemma I described in the previous chapters. Though I present it in my own subjective, individual manner, this way of seeing things grows out of the collective endeavor of radicals in legal education across the country to find a mode of resistance. I don't speak for this group, scattered in places like Boston, Buffalo, Camden, Madison, Miami, Palo Alto, but I do speak from its midst.

* * * * * * *

Legal hierarchy is a typical American phenomenon, rather than something peculiar to law or even to the professions. Law firms and law schools strongly resemble, from the point of view of hierarchy, the other institutions of our society, including state bureaucracies, service corporations, and industry. The relationship between legal education and law practice is typical of relationships between the parts of the total hierarchical structure that have strong functional, input-output links. And, the ideology of legal hierarchy is no more than a specialized application of the general meritocratic ideology of American society.

Reproduction of Hierarchy   85

An accurate description of the total hierarchical structure
of which legal hierarchy is a part would have to take into account the following traits: First, the structure is diamond
shaped rather than dichotomous or pyramidal, with more people
in the middle than at the top or the bottom.

Second, at a given level, regionalism and the division of
labor, along with race and sex, create sharp cleavages in
tastes, capacities, and values.

Third, the whole is organized into corporate cells, each
of which includes people from different strata doing different
tasks; to some extent people identify with "their" corporate
cell rather than with their class position.

Fourth, each of the corporate cells roughly mirrors the
internal hierarchical arrangement of all the others, and of the
hierarchy viewed as a totality.

Fifth, every one of these internally hierarchical elements
supports by analogy the legitimacy of each of the others, while
at the same time contributing to the functioning of the whole
through what it produces.

Sixth, there are no "primary" or "fundamental" parts of
this structure, no part that is "material" as opposed to "superstructural," and every part is constituted by a complex blend-
ing of the use or threat of force with ideological cooptation.

If we see the larger social world this way, we have to give up the notion that the total system of hierarchy has a powerful structure that is the key both to understanding it and to changing it. This means renouncing the characteristic theoretical claims both of orthodox marxist and of left liberal critics of hierarchy, since neither the organized working class nor the state has a privileged position in the totality.

Orthodox marxist theorists argue that the proletariat is a class with an unequivocal interest in revolution and the particular organizational strengths and strategic position necessary to achieve it. But in the modern structure of hierarchy, the proletariat has ceased to exist, at least in the 19th century sense. Those at the very bottom of the diamond of hierarchy are few in numbers, demoralized, and functionally marginal to the totality. Welfare mothers, illegal immigrants and urban squatters simply are not a revolutionary class.

The force of an analysis based on the distinction between productive workers and idle capitalists has faded along with the proletariat itself. The main problem is not how to expropriate the capitalist class, but how to overcome the unjust and unnecessary inequality of power and reward among those who work or want to work, and the patterns of behavior that reenforce and legitimate that inequality generation after generation. (I'm not saying that capitalists don't exist, or that they don't oppress others, but just that this is only one in the list of modes of oppression, and no longer, if it ever was, the central one.)

In both liberal and marxist theory, the state has a crucial role, in each case as a deus ex machina. Sometimes, the notion is that the state represents the interests of the ruling class of capitalists and represses, using brute force or clever concessions or both, attempts by the masses to free themselves of exploitation. Sometimes the problem is that the rules of the game set up in the legal system are biased or discriminatory, and the goal of political activism is to change them so that they will be appropriately neutral among the warring groups of civil society.

The problem with both these points of view is that the state has blurred into the rest of society just as the proletariat has blurred into the middle class. Many distinct interests, not remotely reducible to "capital", have appropriated hunks of state power and pursue their goals through "public" institutions at the local, metropolitan, regional, state and federal levels. The things these public institutions do are no longer at all easy to distinguish from the things the other corporate cells in the hierarchy do. There are no distinguishable state functions that aren't sometimes performed by private organizations, and no private functions that aren't sometimes performed by the state. There are dozens of functions that we don't think of as distinctly one or the other, such as providing transportation or communications.

This means that the state doesn't exist any more than the proletariat does. There are people loosely organized in cells, internally hierarchical, linked in input-output relationships with other cells, and the cells that are conventionally categorized together as "the state" could just as plausibly be divided up and recombined in a dozen other ways. It is not even true that we can say the state's output is "suppression of change" or "adjusting the system to crises," since sometimes the different cells arbitrarily labelled "public" do this and sometime they do the opposite, fostering change and destabilizing other parts of the system. The nominally public cells sometimes regulate other aspects of the system but are themselves regulated as well.

In this view, rather than a system powefully structured by the relationship between workers and capitalists, or by the directive strategies of a state, there is a system without any overarching logic--a congeries of roughly similarly patterned elements which are just there, as opposed to flowing out of an integrating concept or factual relation. To say that the system continues in existence is just to say that most of the corporate cells manage to keep going, on their own but relying on and competing with other cells, sometimes joining in coalitions consciously designed to protect interests of the whole system, sometimes refusing to do so. As a matter of fact, the system has survived and adapted, but that didn't have to happen, and there's nothing to guarantee it will continue to happen.

Reproduction of Hierarchy 89

The phrase "reproduction of hierarchy" (as opposed, say, to "perpetuation of oppression") is meant to convey this perspective--the notion that the system is dis-integrated, although not utterly chaotic. It is an organic metaphor--the system is there because it is reborn piecemeal in each generation, rather than being a conceptually graspable something that outsiders (capital, the ruling class, the state) impose and maintain. If you want to explain the status quo, you have to go into the details of how people, new people in each generation, learn to be little white middle class males, teen-aged black welfare mothers living in public housing projects, and so forth. There's more to it than the state, or one's relation to the means of production. There's all the stuff that, in the case of lawyers, I tried to describe in the chapters on the contributions of legal education to the hierarchies of the legal profession.

If a band of revolutionaries, or a band of moderate liberal reformers, were to seize some important hunk of the state, or even every cell arguably a part thereof, they would be incapable, for all their apparent power, of changing most of what is detestable about our system. The hateful stuff is embedded in the hundreds of thousands of little behavior patterns and implicit training programs that constitute the totality. The liberal state is too weak and the totalitarian state too strong for the task of transformation. Where what we long for is free self-determination within every cell, the liberal state can only regulate the powerful while the totalitarian state can only tell us what to do and not to do.

The revolution that counts is the revolution of civil society, a revolution within each cell, from the shop floor to the
nuclear family to the office to the classroom. Though revolutionary decrees, or administrative regulations, would be helpful, they would also be dangerous. An official, public, governmental revolution risks impotence unless its authors are
willing to take it very far indeed, at which point they risk
degeneration into revolutionary dictatorship.

But if we have to abandon the notion of the state as a
transformative agent, we can also let go the fear that the state
can somehow repress any attempt at fundamental change.
There is no process of secular "rationalization" that slowly im-
plants order so deeply that freedom becomes unimaginable.
The occasions of freedom run like veins of ore through what
seem the most monolithic institutions; they exist in pockets and
interstices that escape even a very careful eye. And all occasions of freedom are fundamental: just as there is no core or
basic relation or logic of the system, so there is no single,
fragile heart of the opposition.

What has happened is a simultaneous blurring of lines between classes and institutions that were once distinct (at least
in theory) and a diffusion of social power through the hierarchy that has made it, paradoxically, at once more stable and
more vulnerable. The system runs on training for hierarchy,
on the threat and reality of physical violence against dissen-

Reproduction of Hierarchy　　　　　　　　　　　　91

ters, and on everyone's sense that those above them will never
permit change, while those below them would take everything
if given half a chance. This sense is confirmed, falsely, by
myriad everyday events, from the firing of workers for trying
to organize unions to ghetto riots. It is confirmed for law
students by the admissions process, competition for grades,
relations with teachers and fellow students, and the placement
process. But it is only a "sense," a false sense.

Those at the top of the various hierarchies--dispersed as
they are in the cellular structure--have no better theory of
why they are in power and how to stay there than the left has
of how to get them out. If battle lines were to be drawn, no
one knows where they would fall. Where they fell in fact
would depend on millions of decisions by individuals and
groups animated by conflicting motives of loyalty and hatred of
the existing order, hope and fear about the future. But it is
quite possible that battle lines will never be drawn, that the
struggle will remain diffuse, pervasive without being organized, and that might not be a bad thing. If there is no revolutionary class and the state is just an institution among many,
to seize power means to transform society piecemeal.

*　*　*　*　*　*　*

People differently situated in the structure of hierarchy
receive radically different shares of the social product and

exercise radically different degrees of social power. But their lives differ just as profoundly on dimensions that have nothing to do with the quantitative issue, How Much? Class, sex and race, along with the more particular cultures of regions and corporate organizations, generate differences in tastes, capacities and values. The judgment that shares of power and reward are unequal and unjust is therefore a complex one. It can't be based on a concept like exploitation, since there is no "natural" value for anyone's labor and no one has an abstract right to receive any particular thing or to live any particular life.

It has to be based on the belief that everyone has the capacity for the most valuable forms of experience, and on the processual belief that people can and should collectively determine the conditions of collective life. These beliefs cannot be grounded in reason, as reason is commonly understood, nor is it possible to resolve their contradictions otherwise than in practice, but that is not to say that they are arbitrary. Because the existing system of hierarchy denies their validity and frustrates their realization, we should abolish it.

The left should not pretend that it has a solution, especially a proposed institutional solution to the problem of how substantive (not formal) equality of power and reward can exist in a world where people are different from one another, irreducibly and also valuably different. A left movement bent

Reproduction of Hierarchy   93

on transforming the system of hierarchy would have to choose,
over and over again, what meaning to give to equality, both in
reward and in power. Because the system creates groups of
people with different tastes, values and capacities, this process of choice would involve distinguishing and then accepting
and rejecting the tastes, values and capacities of groups.

It may appear that this is less problematic with respect to
capacities than with respect to values. We all recognize that
one is more likely to learn to read and write easily, and to do
abstract forms of instrumental reasoning, if one has had a
middle or upper middle class education as opposed to a lower
middle or working class education. It is not that hierarchical
position guarantees competence, or that a lower position pre-
cludes it. But it is clear that this system produces enormous
differences in actual reading, writing and calculating capacities. These differences count. One is worse off if one
doesn't have the capacities than if one does.

And yet to designate literacy or calculating ability as
something everyone should have, would still involve a choice
--to risk the atrophy of <u>other</u> cultural capacities for expression and interaction that have failed in the past, for whatever
reason, to hold their own in competition with the highly cognitive style of the Western bourgeoisie. It is hard to imagine
a world in which this kind of issue would not cause conflict,
and there are no answers that flow simply from the idea of

equality. The struggle against hierarchy has to be understood as a struggle for the recognition and then the resolution in practice of contradictions of this kind, rather than as a struggle to impose a solution derived analytically from a political philosophy.

With respect to cultural values, the situation is similar. All social classes generate practices and artifacts that we think of as "their own." These are sometimes adopted by other groups; sometimes they become universal values of a culture and transcend class. This might be said of rock music in the 1960's, or of the novel form, or of the conception of honor of the feudal aristocracy. But even where the culture of a class remains very much its own, it is never its own creation. Classical music is unimaginable without the eighteenth century artisan class, or without lower middle class musicians. Hegel's philosophy is unimaginable without his servants, modern American black culture without nineteenth century white slave masters.

The left in power would have to judge the values of social classes, however ambiguously identified, and pick and choose among them, whether we liked it or not, as we do whenever we choose to act in the world. Values conflict and even when they don't, life is short. Anyone who wields social power, including all lawyers and all law teachers, constantly influences the choices of others, and no amount of respect for diversity

Reproduction of Hierarchy   95

can exempt from responsibility for that influence. The situation would be no different in an ideal democracy--for citizens to be equal they must be engaged with one another, and engagement implies the acceptance of influence.

To meet this responsibility, we have to come to grips with questions like, "Is it permissible for lawyers, by offering easy divorce, protection against wife beating, access to contraception, abortion, and joint child custody, to destabilize working class family life, in the name of a conception of women's liberation whose origins are predominantly in middle and upper middle class culture?" I would answer "yes" to this question, for this time and place, but insist that there is an element of class violence involved, a choice by one group to impose its values on another.

This is not to assert that white working class people overwhelmingly or even by a majority oppose abortion or easy divorce or favor wife beating, or that the "true consciousness" of the white working class is sexist. None of this is true. But in order to make choices of this kind honestly, it seems to me one must recognize that, in the main, the flow of energy in the women's movement has been downward through the class hierarchy. And that this is an accomplishment, the creation of value, by the bourgeoisie, just as was true of the building of the productive capacity of capitalism. The struggle against hierarchy has to be a struggle within the movement itself to recognize and then resolve in practice issues of this kind, however painful they may be.

Our inability to derive a practical program by analysis from a political philosophy renders the whole enterprise of social transformation problematic, when looked at from the point of view of rationalist theories, like the belief in natural rights or the version of Marxism that sees collective ownership of the means of production as the purpose of revolution. But even without a theory in the strong sense claimed by earlier radical movements, even though we have to make it up as we go along, it is something to know what one is against. At least in a limited sense, the negation of hierarchy generates an affirmative value, even a universal value.

The power to create new forms of human association in discontinuous constitutive moments and in slow evolutionary practice, is as great a human power as that of creating material sustenance from nature or that of encoding meaning in artifacts. When that power is dispersed through a hierarchy of roles, and every person is constrained, by fear of falling lower and the illusory hope of happiness higher up, to give themselves over to those roles, the power is still exercised. It is exercised, but no one exercises it. Instead of the experience of creation, of freedom, there is the experience of bondage, though the social totality is transformed in the process of that bondage.

Reproduction of Hierarchy   97

What the left offers is liberation from the constraints of hierarchy, the process of bondage, through the conscious practice of group self-determination, in every area of life. There is no one who lacks an objective interest in this form of liberation.

Chapter Eight

Strategy

Given its peculiar structure--the analogy of the parts one to another and of each part to the totality, and the reproduction within each part of the energy that animates the whole (i.e., the absence of a "heart" of the system)--to transform the system of hierarchy by the reappropriation of the power of social creation would be to transform every cell. This can only be done cell by cell, until we reach the critical point at which the interconnectedness of the system makes it possible to develop it as a whole toward a new unity.

To the extent this description is correct, it is not only possible but also meaningful to resist anywhere and at any time--at upper middle class dinner parties and at the bank as well as in law school classrooms, faculty meetings, on the as-

Reproduction of Hierarchy   99

sembly line and in welfare offices. It is valid because wher-
ever you are situated, the system of hierarchy maims you. It
is valid because the other people situated as you are are also
maimed. It is valid because all the different struggles are
connected by the analogy of the structures of the different
cells, and therefore reenforce one another.

Because hierarchy is constituted as much through ideology as through physical violence, it is meaningful to oppose it
by talking, by joking and refusing to laugh at jokes, through
the elaboration of fantasies as well as through the elaboration
of concrete plans for struggle.

Let me hasten to affirm, O Reader, that not all resistance
is equally heroic, or equally successful, or equally well-con-
ceived, or equally adapted to an overall strategy for turning
resistance into something more. I propose in the next chapter
that law students and teachers should take relatively minor
professional risks. All over the world, workers and peasants
and political activists have risked and lost their lives. There
is a gulf between these two kinds of action, and I have no
desire to minimize it.

But they are nonetheless parts of the same universe, and
we possess no grand theory telling us that actions of one kind
or the other are bound always and everywhere to be futile,
any more than we can know that the most heroic behavior will
be always successful.

Thinking of this kind runs counter to the basic left attitude that the motive of political activity for middle class people
should be compassion for those less fortunate than themselves
and guilt for their complicity in injustice. Nothing could be
further from my intention than to undercut those motives.
But I want to put beside them two others: the sense of loss
and dishonor felt at the alienation of one's own powers through
hierarchy, and the sense of solidarity with others in one's own
social situation who are similarly maimed.

It may have been true for earlier generations of leftists
that to identify oneself with the struggles of the oppressed
necessarily involved a leap out of one's bourgeois identity, a
radical negation as well as a radical affirmation. The mystique
of the bourgeois intellectual who turns utterly against his origins to become a professional revolutionary is still alive today.
It makes it seem, first, that nothing short of this stance is a
meaningful commitment to left politics, and, second, that left
activity directed at people who are compromised by hierarchy,
rather than unequivocally oppressed by it, is suspect a priori.

One can concede the moral significance and accomplish-
ments of those who have followed this path of total negation,
while still affirming that every further development of the
modern system of hierarchy makes it less likely that they can
succeed. It has gradually become clear how much of domination there is in the revolutionary's conception of service, even

Reproduction of Hierarchy   101

where she makes every effort to respect the autonomy of the people she works with.   As the distance between classes has in some ways narrowed, we have become more rather than less aware of how hierarchical position influences every aspect of our social being, so that the simple negation of one's class self, or sexual self, or racial self, comes to seem an impossible, and maybe even an undesirable objective.

The alternative strategy is that of building, cell by cell, an organized left bourgeois intelligentsia that might one day join together with a mass movement for the radical transformation of American society.   The great movements of liberation in the history of the West (and also of the third world) have always had in their service cadres of class turncoats from the intelligentsia, who provided them everything from a few ideas, to some knowledge of tactical use, to leadership itself.   Without such a cadre, it is unlikely that a mass movement could ever be permanently successful in the United States, where ideology is a particularly important instrument of domination and a majority of the population identifies itself as middle class.

In the absence of a mass movement of the left, the way to organize a left intelligentsia is in the workplace, around ideas and around the concrete issues that arise within the bourgeois corporate institutions where the potential members of such an intelligentsia live their lives.   By organization around ideas, I don't mean the propagation of an ideology in the mode of Marxism in Western Europe, or, say, fundamentalist Christianity in the United States. Organizing around ideas means developing a practice of left study, left literature and left debate about philosophy, social theory, and public policy that would give professional, technical and managerial workers the sense of participating in a left community.

Along with workplace organization around ideas there goes organization around the specific issues of hierarchy that are important in the experience of people in these institutions. This has to do with the authoritarian character of day-to-day work organization--with the use of supervisory power. But it also has to do with unspoken professional consensus and with the self-policing or mutual policing of people through the diffuse fear of appearing to be odd or uncooperative. Selection, promotion and pay policies, along with a whole universe of smaller interventions, many of which are merely "social," maintain class/sex/race and also generational and meritocratic stratification within the cells of the hierarchy, while at the same time disciplining everyone to participate in the complex of hierarchical attitudes and behaviors.

It is not possible to organize large, permanent groups of middle class people around issues that primarily affect the working or lower middle class, or the underclass. In so much as it is possible to mobilize professionals, technicians and man-

Reproduction of Hierarchy   103

agers at all, it is either through liberal, reformist strategies that produce episodic large numbers but very shallow commitment, or through sectarianism. Organizing people around the issue of hierarchy in their own work and personal lives, in a way that is neither modeled on the "party" nor on the liberal interest coalition, promises a slow but potentially much more solid long term process of creation, capable of linking up eventually with mass protest against the total structure of hierarchy.

Finally, bourgeois intellectuals of left politics ought to direct a substantial part of their energy at combatting their own experience of oppression. Even if one could not expect that this would produce over time an important contribution to a national left movement, and even if one expected the rewards in terms of better theory to be negligible, bourgeois left intellectuals ought to try to transform their cell in the hierarchy so that they themselves, and those with whom they live and work, have better lives.

What this means is that lawyers can have and should have workplace struggles, no matter where they are situated in the hierarchy of the bar, and whether or not they are actively engaged in political law practice. For law students and law teachers, it means that it is important to have a law school struggle, even if they are spending most of their time on extra-curricular activities that support oppressed people.

It is naive to think that law school can somehow be experienced outside the structure of hierarchy in which it is embedded, that one could treat it as a place to get training in
how to oppose hierarchy without having to contend with it in
one's own life. And it is a cop-out to respond to the presence
of hierarchy in life at law school by blaming the corruption of
law students, or by blaming the ruling class for the diabolical
intensity of the pressures it brings to bear on them.

If you can't find ways to oppose hierarchy in your routine institutional life at school, it is unlikely (though of course
not impossible) that you will bring to activity on behalf of
people lower down in the hierarchy anything like your full
potential power as an activist or organizer or mere supporter.

This point of view is not at all revolutionary: it has nothing to do with preparations for a violent mass uprising or a
coup d'etat, and it is certainly not based on a theory that
capitalism is doomed by its own internal contradictions to succumb to the rising proletariat. On the other hand, what I am
proposing doesn't fit the usual mold of reformism either.

First, it involves risk taking, insubordination, defiance--
in a word, rebellion. It is intensely difficult for a member of
the American middle class meritocratic elite to behave in ways
that presuppose and affirm the invalidity of the existing structure of hierarchy. Because hierarchy is bred so deep into our

Reproduction of Hierarchy 105

bones, there is something shocking, almost parricidal, in the moment when you actually do something that clearly opposes it.

Second, the premise of this strategy is that we should go as far as possible toward the total dismantling of the existing system. The idea is that our society is rotten through and through, so that no adjustment of the rules of the game to make them fairer, or to make hierarchy more socially rational, would be enough. The demand is for a new society.

Third, this strategy is based on the idea that reformism is in fact a hopeless endeavor. Once one accepts this idea, there is no reason at all to sacrifice the long term goal of building a movement for radical transformation to short term gains. It's important to take short term gains when they're offered, but only because it's nice to win something occasionally, and because successful coalitions get one access to people who may be converted to more radical commitments.

It sometimes seems to me that when left law students heap scorn on their contemporaries, seeing them as at once weak, corrupt and brainwashed, and affirm that the only form of meaningful activity is that involving the working class or some other group much worse off than themselves, they are preparing the way for their own demobilization. What they see as real politics is either incredibly difficult (if it is actually revolutionary) or unlikely to make half the difference promised (if it's liberal reformist). The politics they reject, the politics directed at the cell in the structure of hierarchy in which they will live their lives, is easier, for all its moral ambiguities, but you can't do it except by doing it.

The upshot of very high standards of what counts as real political action, in a system in which that kind of action is hard to come by, may be that leftists use their "hard" attitude as a backhanded justification for passivity. This seems today a more serious danger than that syndical workplace struggle by law students and law teachers would drain energy away from the struggles of the less privileged. In that spirit, I have some suggestions about how law students and law teachers can organize themselves to resist within their schools.

Chapter Nine

The Law School Study Group

The core of a law school organizing strategy should be
the left study group. You stand up one day at the end of
class and say, "Anyone interested in forming a left study
group, to deal with questions about what's going on in school
and to connect up with other people doing left things in the
law, should come to a meeting tonight at X p.m." Or you put
a notice on the classroom blackboard, or xerox a flyer.

Not many people will show up, probably, but probably
some people will. What they'll have in common, more likely
than not, is a sense of outrage at the authoritarian style of at
least one first year teacher, and a vague uneasiness that
somehow the first year curriculum is heavily ideological even
though no one can say exactly how. Then there is the sense
that law school means selling out, and that one has to find
somehow an extra-curricular activity that will keep one in
touch with one's ideals.

A group of people loosely united by sentiments like these develops into an organization by talking about their law school experiences, reading texts together, and trying to relate the texts to their institutional situation.   There is a fairly substantial critical literature about the subject matter of the first year curriculum.   A book like <u>The Politics of Law</u>, or Horwitz's <u>Transformation of American Law</u>, may be a good place to begin reading together.   Texts of this kind give the group a direct relevance to day-to-day life as a law student.   But it makes sense to read general left social theory as well, whether it be Marx on the Jewish Question, or maybe Genovese's discussion of the law of slavery, or E.P. Thompson's of legality in 18th century England.*

At the same time, it is important to link up with other people who are concerned with the issue of hierarchy in your institution and the surrounding community.   There will almost certainly be at least one professor who is at least vaguely sympathetic, and he or she may be able to provide support of various kinds.   If there isn't a local student chapter of the National Lawyers Guild, it makes sense to think about starting one, and to use that activity as a way to get in touch with left members of the local bar.   Another possibility is a speakers program, through which you bring to the school local or more distant left practitioners, left law professors or non-legal left academics and organizers.

---

*For fuller references, see the suggested reading list, page 124 below.

None of these activities can be expected to convert a large segment of the institution to resistance to hierarchy, but once they get started they are likely to build slowly, and you will find yourself with some kind of place in school politics. What one does with this possibility of influence depends on circumstances--the contingent ebb and flow of school issues. But there are three kinds of project that are likely to be useful at some point.

One of these is the organization of the study group to perform an act of resistance of some kind in the authoritarian classroom.   This tactic is completely dependent on solidarity of at least three people, who are willing to support each other aggressively when the teacher pulls out the big guns to silence the first person he or she perceives as disruptive.   It involves a conscious intention to stand up to student pressure to shut up and let the teacher "get on with it."   But the actual act of resistance could be any one of a range of things, from a formal request that the teacher not tell sexist jokes, through a challenge to the exclusion from the syllabus of the politically delicate aspects of the subject matter, to the refusal to go along with the ritual of the socratic method--for example, by refusing to attack another student's position, or insisting on the right to "pass" when called upon.

It is difficult to pull off an action of this kind.   It requires those who do it to blend two motives and two psycho-

logical styles that are likely to seem incompatible. On one side
is the element of "witness," the tapping of the pure impulse of
rebellion. One does it because one can't do otherwise, in
spite of the fact that it is terrifying to make a public spectacle
of yourself in a school classroom, and in spite of the probabi-
lity that the teacher and your fellow students will squash you
flat.

On the other side, and operating at the same time, there
should be a cold calculation of political effectiveness. You
don't want to get thrown out of school; you shouldn't do it in
a way that will get you thrown out, or irredeemably compro-
mise your chances of getting a degree and a job. And you
should have in mind, in conceiving the form and content of the
action, some actual audience of students or others for whom it
will have a meaning, even though they will sit there shivering
in their boots if you go down in flames, and even though they
will, at least initially, recoil in horror if it works.

A second kind of project, which doesn't require such a
volatile mixture of rebellion and calculation, is to propose a
change in the content of the curriculum so as to make it at
once less politically biased to the right and less of an engine
of incapacitation for alternative forms of practice. Again,
there are a range of possibilities. There is the constitutional
law teacher who spends almost all his time on the commerce
clause, and no time to speak of on substantive issues of racism

Reproduction of Hierarchy 111

and sexism. There is the general bias against confronting the political and ideological character of law study. The placement process is most likely a funnel rather than a means to maximum choice. Every school ought to offer courses that will practically empower students to practice law in a small, new law firm doing neighborhood law practice with an activist political component.

A third initiative is to demand that your school operate a legal services clinic for poor people. There are many possible models, but the essential point is that the school and its students should recognize an obligation to provide legal service free to some specific geographic community or other identifiable group. Under the best circumstances, a clinic can concretize the kind of politics I have been talking about here in several different ways, and it is therefore an ideal issue for student agitation and organized left involvement. Moreover, most existing clinical programs are agressively apolitical, so the fact that a school already has one doesn't mean that there's nothing to fight about.

First, clinical legal education has been one of the sources of teaching innovation implicitly (at least) in opposition to the authoritarianism and sterility of the traditional law school classroom. Second, a functioning legal aid clinic brings students into direct contact with the lives of working class and welfare class people of all races and nationalities; the shock of that experience creates at least a potential for radicalization.

Third, the daily operation of a clinic constantly raises political issues that are central to the existence of a middle class left intelligentsia. There is the choice between a paternal and an egalitarian style of relationship between lawyer and client; the choice between cooptation by the local system for the administration of justice and a strategy which is at least potentially a radical challenge to that system; and the choice between being invisible in relation to the organized parts of the community served and entering into local politics. There are also difficult and important substantive issues of legal strategy: should the clinic aggressively enforce the housing code at the risk of speeding abandonment or gentrification? Are divorce cases "merely personal," or at the core of a feminist politics of legal services?

These three initiatives--an action against the authoritarian classroom, a proposal about the curriculum and the placement process, and a legal services clinic--touch directly on law school and life as a lawyer. Only the third has an equally direct relation to the politics of the society at large. Study groups should at least make an effort to find local labor union insurgents, radical feminist networks and activist groups in the black community. Law students may have something to offer them in the form of legal work, and they have a lot to gain from contact with them. The group shouldn't see itself as existing for their sake, but it shouldn't let itself be isolated either. The slogan of resistance anywhere, any time,

Reproduction of Hierarchy   113

on any issue, doesn't imply that one should resist all alone,
and it <u>may</u> be the case that there are specific actions in the
"real world" through which law students can do more for the
cause of the left than they can do by concentrating on their
own issues.   There is no way to know about this a priori.

* * * * * * * *

   In groups of the kind I've been talking about, there seem
almost always to be conflicts of personality, moments of faction-
alism in which abstract disagreements, about the wording of a
statement or the choice of a tactic, seem to mask the same man-
euvering for dominance and the same petty defensiveness that
the group is fighting against.   One way to react to this is to
quit in disgust.   You can always conclude that hierarchy and
the conflicts it generates are "inevitable," and that the best
one can do is to avoid any group situation in which the possibility of actually exercising power brings them to the surface.
Another kind of response is to decide that without discipline,
nothing happens but chaos and demoralization, so that the
group should become a formal organization with lines of command of some kind.

Neither of these responses makes sense, at least not if one accepts the main lines of the analysis of this essay. The left study group is a cell of the total social organism, like the school within which it arises. And since hierarchical behavior is bred into us in all the complex ways I've been trying to describe, we bring it with us into any group we participate in. You shouldn't join a left study group in order to escape from hierarchy, but in order to transform it. If this is to occur, the group has to confront it and thrash it out, and then confront it again and thrash it out again. If that fails, then it makes sense to dissolve the group (or just walk away from it) and try again with other people, using what one has learned as the basis for a new start.

For example, the vagueness of left groups in their early stages encourages the flowering of neurotic scene-stealers. They bring their agendas from somewhere else (childhood, it often seems). They insist, against flaccid resistance, that everyone hear out their obliquely self-praising monologue, or stereotypical protest about the absence of the working class, or about how the men dominated the meeting (there were only two women and one of them hasn't even tried to speak until she makes this speech).

This person drives everyone else crazy--they want to kill, or at least to leave. But the unacceptable violence of this reaction, along with uncertainty about one's place in the group, genuine adherence to the norm of openness, fear of what the scene-stealer will do in retaliation to anyone who interrupts him--all these make it look to him and to everyone else as though there is general acquiescence, even polite interest in what is going on.   There will be no second meeting.

Ignoring such people doesn't work--that's how they get their air time in the first place.   It's better to get up your courage to say in a calm and warm but unmistakably dismissive tone of voice that this is a tangent.   As the group breathes a sigh of relief, someone who detested the scene-stealing will speak up for the scene-stealer, out of fear that you are trying to establish dictatorial powers.   But maybe there won't be any more monologues, at least for a while.   (There is another version of this story: in an energyless, drifting group, the scene-stealer may be the only person searching loyally and stubbornly for the conditions that would permit him to be committed to the enterprise--searching precisely for the group in which someone will confront him rather than suffering then avoiding him.)

There are also groups in which there seems at first to be intense competition for leadership among half the members, along with passivity, or persistent requests to "get on with it," from the other half.   In the scramble for air time, the aggressive interrupt the passive (who become more so), put each other down, and appeal persuasively to the group as a whole.

116   Legal Education and the

It can be liberating to realize that this has nothing to do with
doing things: the scramblers have no intention of making a
plan, spending the time to carry it out, and taking the blame
or even the credit for the outcome.   It's about pecking order,
period.

     This means that whether you were initially one of the
scramblers or one of the "let's get on with it" faction, there
isn't much standing in the way of just starting to do something, letting the others make up their own minds how they
feel about it.   If you seem about to do some real work, others
will almost certainly join you, and decisions begin to emerge
from the collective without the need for any resolution of the
burning issues the scramblers were using to set the pecking
order.   When the question is "who can draw?" and "how do we
pay for the xeroxing," some, but not all scramblers will fade
away, as will the passive ones who never really wanted to "get
on with it," but enjoyed being the people the scramblers
fought over.

     Struggling to make the group a prefiguration of what it is
struggling for is not the same thing as struggling against leadership per se.   But there are no formulae by which one can
tell in advance at what point, through what words or acts,
leadership has degenerated into mere hierarchy.   Attempts to
state a set of principles by which to distinguish between
"good" and "bad" leaders break down in the same way that

attempts to formulate a method of legal reasoning break down. There is an irreducible element of intuition, luck and grace both in leading well and in deciding when it's going so badly that it's time to rebel or leave.

It is a good maxim that leadership is a function demanded by particular tasks, not an office or a "personality type." Responsibilities should be diffused and rotated, so that peoples' capacities develop through group work, and there should be checks and balances. But when someone is doing something well and no one feels they threaten to turn their performance into illegitimate power, it makes sense to reap the benefit of their expertise.

It is a good maxim that the atmosphere of group discussion should be such that people can change their positions without feeling they have been humiliated, and refuse to change them without feeling they have left the group. Where those with factual power of leadership demand that it be celebrated through formal acknowledgements of error or even much more subtle bendings of the knee, the group has lost its commitment to openness. On the other hand, there is such a thing as mindless pluralism in which no one ever dares tell anyone else they're talking nonsense. It seems to me better to manage as best one can using this kind of mushy calculus than to resort to the formalization of procedures and the rhetoric of discipline.

*   *   *   *   *   *   *

A final aspect of study group practice is utopian think-ing. By this I mean not the attempt to discover an ideal form of social arrangement which would put an end to historical struggle and uncertainty, but a practice of formulating demands so as to reveal the hidden ideological presuppositions of institutional life. An effective utopian proposal honors all the "practical" constraints that center-liberal administrators appeal to when asked to explain the way their institutions work, so that it can't be dismissed as flatly impossible, or beyond the capacities of those who would have to carry it out.

At the same time, an effective utopian proposal has no chance at all of being adopted (at least in the near future) be-cause it violates the unspoken conservative norms that guide administration in fact, if not in name. It should represent small scale and middle term, rather than "final" programmatic thinking, based on a rough assumption that the world outside the institution in question remains unchanged, and subject to revision in every detail as the process of left study and action clarifies our thinking about how we might actually change things if we had some measure of power.

This kind of work has value in the rhetorical battle against those who alternately portray the left as hopelessly visionary and as practically unoriginal. But its deeper impor-tance is as an aspect of the life of the group. People ought to quarrel and then try tentatively for closure about what to do, about whether a given proposal would make things better or make them even worse. It helps in figuring out what's really wrong with the way things are, even if there is little chance of carrying out any radical change in the short run. It is crucial to form coalitions based on a relatively vague consensus that things should be different, and it is a mistake to carry programmatic thinking to the point of hardness where it excludes potential allies. But it is never too early to start building a much sharper consensus about what we would do if we could.

What follows is an example of this kind of thinking: a summary of a proposal to the Harvard curriculum committee written in 1980. It is addressed to an elite private law school, and doesn't confront the overall organization of legal education. (For example, it doesn't take up the idea of random assignment of teachers and equalization of financial resources as a way to abolish the hierarchy of schools.) But even with these allowances, it already seems to me dated and inadequate, mainly because it doesn't pay enough explicit attention to the modelling of hierarchy through teacher-student and student-student relationships. I offer it not as a blueprint, but as a contribution to a dialogue that is already under way, and that will gain depth and sharpness with the growth of our power.

120   Legal Education and the

Utopian Proposal

A. The New Model Curriculum

A required program to be taken in a prescribed sequence over two years and one summer, covering all basic doctrinal areas and skills, clinical experience and interdisciplinary study, followed by a diversified third year.

1. The Rules/Skills Course: An aggregate of three semesters of programmed instruction in doctrine, including learning rule systems and learning the skills of case manipulation, rule manipulation and pro/con policy argument, conveyed through "cases and materials," computer learning machine exercises, facilitation classes run by faculty members, video-taped lecture series, and tutorial.

2. The Clinical Program: A required sequence of clinical experiences, spaced over the two years, and aggregating one semester and one two-month summer stint, covering most practical and ethical aspects of law practice, using simulations, extensive legal writing, small scale experience in hearing-type settings, and two months in the school's large Legal Clinic modelled after a university teaching hospital.

37

3 The Legal Decision Course: A required course running parallel to the rules/skills course, meeting three or four hours a week, covering materials in history, jurisprudence, economics, sociology of law and the legal profession, social psychology, social theory and political philosophy, closely integrated with both doctrinal and clinical study, and taught so that each student is exposed to two formally distinguished "streams," one representing the left and the other the right political tendencies in approaching the materials.

4. The Third Year: A third year resembling what we have now, with no formal requirements and great faculty flexibility in deciding what to teach, but with the addition of three options, each of which could take up some or all of a student's time: a Research Institute, advanced work in the Clinic, and concentration in one or more practice specialties or conceptually defined fields of study.

B. The Law School as a Counterhegemonic Enclave

This is a set of proposals designed to reduce illegitimate hierarchy and alienation within the school, and to reduce or reverse the school's role in promoting illegitimate hierarchy and alienation in the bar and the country at large.

1. Admissions: There should be a test designed to establish minimal skills for legal practice and then a lottery for ad-

mission to the school; there should be quotas within the lottery for women, minorities and working class students. There should be a national publicity campaign about our goal of modifying the social composition of the bar.

2. Hierarchy among Students: A program designed to reduce disparities in educational attainment of students while at law school, through a combination of redesign of the curriculum (see the NMC above) and investment of large sums of money and resources in students at the bottom of the academic hierarchy. Abolition of current law review selection system; modification of the grading system to eliminate perverse incentives; new forms of feedback at all levels.

3. Channeling of Students: A program to give students accurate information about hierarchical and moral realities of different kinds of practice, combined with training designed to give them technical, social and psychological resources necessary for real freedom of choice between large law firms and other kinds of work. Overhaul of the placement system to equalize the chances of competitors of large firms, even at the price of making our graduates less attractive to the large firms. Studies aimed to discover possibilities for viable publicly oriented and small scale practice, including development of proposals for curricular or statutory reform where necessary.

Reproduction of Hierarchy   123

   4. Faculty Hierarchy: Hire most qualified women, minority
and working class candidates until those groups occupy a reasonable number of faculty positions. Abolish the distinction
between tenured and untenured faculty--all tenured or none
tenured. Democratize hiring through an elected appointments
committee with representation of all groups in the school.
Develop a program to reduce existing disparities in teaching
and scholarly capacity of different faculty members, analogous
to the attack on disparities among students.

   5. General School Hierarchy: Equalize all salaries in the
school (including secretaries and janitors), regardless of educational qualifications, "difficulty" of job, or "social contribution." Encourage (without violating the NLRA) the forma-
tion of unions of employees at all hierarchical levels. Faculty
should push for: (a) everyone should have some version of
the faculty's unscheduled work experience, or the faculty
should have less of that experience; (b) the division of labor
should be reduced by adding functions within existing job
classifications and reducing the total number of kinds of jobs;
(c) every person should spend one month per year performing
a job in a different part of the hierarchy from his or her nor-
mal job, and over a period of years everyone should be
trained to do some jobs at each hierarchical level.

124   Legal Education and the

Suggested First Reading List for a Left Study Group

Freeman, A.   Legitimizing Racial Discrimination Through Anti-
    Discrimination Law: A Critical Review of Supreme Court
    Doctrine, 62 Minn. L. Rev. 1049 (1978)

Genovese, E.   Roll, Jordan, Roll: The World the Slaves Made
    (1974) Ch. I

Hay, D. et al.   Albion's Fatal Tree: Crime and Society in
    Eighteenth-Century England (1975) Ch. I

Horwitz, M.   The Transformation of American Law, 1780-1860
    (1977)

Kairys, D., ed.   The Politics of Law: A Progressive Critique
    (1982)

Kennedy, D.   Distributive and Paternalist Motives in Contract
    and Tort Law, with Special Reference to Compulsory
    Terms and Unequal Bargaining Power, 41 Maryland L.
    Rev. 563 (1982)

Klare, K.   Judicial Deradicalization of the Wagner Act and the
    Origins of Modern Legal Consciousness, 1937-1941, 62
    Minn. L. Rev. 265 (1978)

Reproduction of Hierarchy   125

Livingston, D.   Note: 'Round & 'Round the Bramble Bush:
    From Legal Realism to Critical Legal Scholarship, 95
    Harvard L. Rev. 1669 (1982)

Marx, K.   Essay on the Jewish Question [any edition of Marx's
    early works]

Olsen, F.   The Family and the Market: A Study of Ideology
    and Legal Reform, 96 Harvard L. Rev. 1497 (1983)

Parker, R.   The Past of Constitutional Theory and its Future,
    42 Ohio State L. J. 223 (1981)

Thompson, E.P.   Whigs and Hunters: The Origin of the Black
    Act (1975) Ch. 10 § 4.

Unger, R.   Law in Modern Society (1976)

    In the interest of brevity and accessibility, this list
leaves out much of the best of current radical legal scholarship.   Write me (c/o Harvard Law School, Cambridge, MA
02138) for a much longer, free Bibliography of Critical Legal
Studies.

This pamphlet grew out of participation in the Conference on Critical Legal Studies, which was founded in 1977 at a meeting in Madison, Wisconsin. Most of its members are law teachers, law students, lawyers or social scientists. The Conference organizes annual meetings (and sometimes summer workshops) at which people discuss law, legal doctrine and practice, legal education and social theory. The Conference tries to bring together Marxist and non-Marxist radical approaches to law. The Conference Secretary is Mark Tushnet, 1416 Holly St. N.W., Washington, DC 20012. Anyone interested in going to a meeting, becoming a member or being on the mailing list should contact him.

* * * * * * *

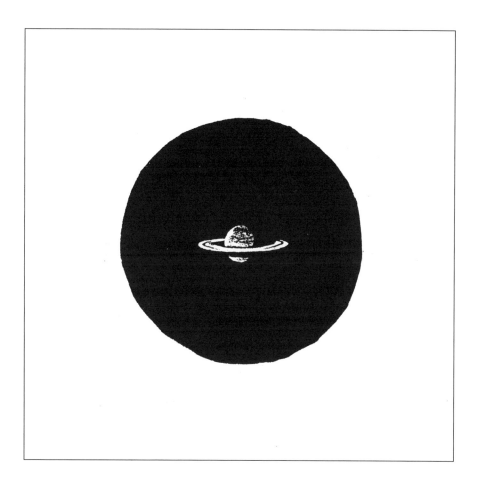

L
E G
A L ★
E D U C
A T I O N
★ A N D ★ T
H E ★ R E P R
O D U C T I
O N ★ O F
★ H I E
R A R
C H
Y

Reproducing the Right Sort of Hierarchy

Paul Carrington

In my youth almost a half-century ago, I attended a school dedicated to the subordination of its students. The teachers made incessant demands on their students. Inadequacies in their performances were publicly observed without pity, and often in the most insulting terms.[1]

We students at that school were almost randomly selected. We did not choose to go there, and indeed, most of us did not want to go to school at all. Certainly none of us relished the incessant demands and insults. We were forced to do what had to be done when it had to be done, and we gradually acquired the habit of prompt obedience.

But we acquired other traits as well. The teachers' seeming inhumanity had at least three redemptive consequences. The most obvious was that it demonstrated their conviction that their work, and hence the work they demanded of their students, was important and possible. They could not have all been that grouchy had they been taking their tasks lightly or had they expected that we would fail no matter how hard we tried.

Second, their gruffness conferred on most of us a valuable sense of survivorship. Most of us succeeded at least marginally at the seemingly important feats required, and they were not easy. Especially for those of us who were not very good students in that school, minimal success was a considerable gratification. To use a term not then known, most of us acquired a new measure of *self-esteem,* derived not from praise by others but from achievement permitting self-praise. In part, this was because failure was obviously possible; a few students who could not achieve minimum standards were sent home.

Finally, the teachers' hateful conduct created among the students a sense of interdependency—they provided their students with a common adversary against whom we could and did respond together. We formed bonds of mutual trust. We became artificial siblings. This was extraordinary, given that our backgrounds of race and class were as different as can be imagined, and that the school had only very recently been racially desegregated.

I was twenty-four years old when I attended that school, and I was a lawyer. Most of my fellow students were nineteen or twenty. My special brothers included a black operator of a shoe-shine stand at the Corpus Christi railroad station, a Hispanic grocery clerk from San Antonio, a black warehouse guard from Oakland, and a Japanese American from Redding who had lived for four years in an internment camp. There were also in my immediate circle a butcher from Las Vegas and a guy who aspired to be a professional golfer. One of them may well have been gay; we did not ask and he did not tell. The school was, of course, basic infantry training, and almost all of us had been selected by our local draft boards. It was my buddy from Corpus Christi who pushed me over the barricade that I was not strong enough to climb. He saved me from additional humiliation and stress, a kind deed I could never have repaid.

From my present perspective, I would have to say that basic infantry training was the most effective educational institution I ever had the opportunity to observe. The Phillips Exeter Academy (from which I was quite appropriately expelled) and the Harvard Law School (from which I was not expelled) made strong impressions on me, and the other schools I attended were also pretty good. But neither Exeter nor Harvard achieved in years what the U.S. Army did in weeks to make adults out of almost all of us involuntary selectees. I have, alas, not kept up with my military brothers, but I am as certain as one can be about such matters that they met the chances of life with measurably greater competence and composure than they would have absent what the army did to and for them in eight short weeks. Happily, I know almost for certain that none of them was ever in military combat.

My respect for what the army did is not linked to any militaristic impulses on my part. I was grateful that the army thought me unpromising as an infantryman and later trained me to type and fill out forms. I was never happier than the day I left active duty as a soldier. But passage of a half-century has not erased my affection for my military buddies, nor has my distaste for the military enterprise prevented me from continuing to admire the drill sergeants (perhaps especially the black WAC) who did their work with such spirit and effect.

In varying degrees, hierarchy is indispensable to all human endeavors entailing organized collaboration. Most that are worthwhile require this. One can draw a picture without hierarchy, but one cannot play in an orchestra. An infantry unit without hierarchy is a mob, and one organized by young Kennedy would, in military combat, have been a suicide pact. Could there be a ballet troupe, a basketball team, a hospital, or an industrial organization of whatever kind in a leftist heaven that excluded hierarchy? Many of our most valued freedoms depend on restraints imposed by hierarchies of one kind or another, and there is therefore nothing inherently wrong with reproducing it. Everything depends on the purpose of a hierarchy and the fitness of its methods to that purpose.

Neither the Yale Law School that the adolescent Kennedy attended nor the Harvard Law School of which he was a member when he protested its reproduction of hierarchy was reproducing hierarchy for its own sake. Both were striving to fit their students for professional work in a world filled with all kinds of hierarchies, many bad but many good.[2] They were, among other objectives, trying to fit their students with the moral and intellectual strength and self-confidence that would enable them to exercise prudent professional judgment in distinguishing good from bad, and to withstand the sometimes horrific stress they would experience in vigorously contested circumstances of whatever sort. Most law teachers then supposed, correctly or not, that treating adult students as immature persons needing emotional nurture and intellectual succor was not the way to prepare them for the moral and intellectual combat that pervades the work of American lawyers. If some of their students found the stress of managing their own professional development objectionable and left the school to pursue a different career, that was not a cause for regret but an indication that the schools were serving their students (perhaps especially the former students who left) and the public well.

In Kennedy's time as a student, the Republic that the faculty expected its students to serve was deeply troubled by the ongoing war in Vietnam. The recriminations of their faculty by students then tell us more about the students' maturity and moral state than they tell us about the faculty. "Never trust anyone over thirty" was a slogan of those times. Teaching anything (left law, right law, or mathematics)[3] in that environment was an uphill struggle.

The problem of student mistrust was compounded by the arrival in law schools in numbers first of students of color, then of women, many of whom were quick to suppose that teachers were motivated by an ambition to humiliate them. It is possible that many of the women were "hard-wired" to need and thus demand mentoring relationships that law teachers of that time were not equipped to supply. As a consequence of the efforts of law teachers to accommodate student mistrust and demands for nurture, law school became almost everywhere less stressful, and students were less frequently required to participate actively and competitively in their own instruction.

If Kennedy's teachers were right in their assumptions that they were not merely instructing students in law but also preparing them for professional work as lawyers, and that professional work is in almost all its forms competitive and stressful and often laden with moral ambiguities, the reforms effected in response to the mistrust of their students may have been counterproductive. Law school graduates may have been less well prepared than they might have been for the professional work they sought opportunities to perform. And they may have had less moral autonomy of the sort enabling them to withstand the corruption and moral squalor that is the stuff of human conflict, with which lawyers must deal.

I do not contend that the particular lawyers who later helped the accountants shred Enron documents would have performed more admirably had they been better educated in law school. I reject the arrogant utterance of Professor Felix Frankfurter that "lawyers are what the law schools make them."[4] The opposite would be far more accurate. Steven Pinker has recently published a thorough refutation of the widely shared premise that our children, or even our law students, are blank slates on whom we can write a message of our choosing.[5] Mostly, students, even law students, get their morals from their peers. If Enron's lawyers grew up among neighbors and attended schools and universities with fellow students who measured one another by such superficialities as their annual earnings, without regard for their professional integrity or the worthiness of the services they performed, no professional school could do very much to change that. Nevertheless, Kennedy's teachers may not have been wrong to suppose that moral education is possible. And moral education may be the most important and enduring consequence of good *professional* training in law.

If law teachers today were to seek to prepare their students to withstand the moral squalor they are certain to encounter in performing legal services, how might they pursue that goal? They might seek to foster in their students the gratification that comes from earned self-respect, derived from surviving rigorous demands with little help from intellectual and moral nursemaids, in the hope that the moral and intellectual autonomy thus developed might be put, at least sometimes, to good public use. Would a law school guided by such aims resemble basic infantry training? Maybe a little.

Or maybe it would bear more resemblance to the law school that featured the teaching of Edward "Bull" Warren, whose legendary antics recorded in the lore of the Harvard Law School provided the anecdotes in *Paper Chase*.[6] The school in which he taught took form in the late nineteenth century in response to the idea of Charles Eliot, Harvard's president, who predicted that if law school were made long and hard, the most promising professional students would be attracted by the challenge and opportunity to elevate themselves within the social and professional hierarchy. In the academic marketplace of the nineteenth century, Eliot's idea was a resounding success. Accordingly, the Bull's students were attracted by his sometimes brutal manners. He wrote an autobiography entitled *Spartan Education* in which he expressed the aim of providing his students with the moral and emotional toughness needed to perform important professional service.[7] It was no part of Warren's objective to train students to be weak subordinates in morally corrupt hierarchies, as the young Kennedy seems to have supposed his teachers were doing. Students who survived the Bull were more likely, the Bull thought, to insist on thinking for themselves. His students might also have shared a sense that what they had achieved was important, and perhaps not merely to themselves. And they might have tended to bond with their classmates as co-professionals.

I have actually known quite a few of Bull Warren's students because my father was one of them, and over the years I met many of his classmates. I never had occasion to discuss with any of them their reactions to the Bull. I wonder how he might have scored on student evaluations of his teaching. All his students whom I met, except my father, were in their seniority when I met them. Some were rather pompous, self-seeking persons who might, as best I could tell, have been the sort of lawyers who would have shredded Enron documents without a blink, at least if well paid to do so. But others I knew were morally formidable and autonomous persons who would have participated in such a desperate act only after exercising independent and critical moral judgment and reaching the unlikely conclusion that the world would be a better place if the documents were shredded.

My assessment is not based merely on my intuitive reading of their characters. Dean Acheson,[8] for one, had the moral starch in 1937 to resign as undersecretary of the Treasury because of his belief that President Franklin Roosevelt's monetary policy was morally reprehensible. In 1948, he (with Secretary Marshall) gave President Harry Truman the very unwelcome advice that recognition of a Zionist state would result in a permanent state of undeclared war between the United States and the Muslim world. In 1949, he improvidently stood up for Alger Hiss. In 1951, he stood up to Joseph McCarthy. My father's roommate, Claude Cross, practiced in Boston for many years and exhibited his moral toughness when he undertook the defense of Alger Hiss. One may question Cross's judgment if he lied on his client's behalf, but one cannot question his moral toughness.[9] Raeburn Green practiced in St. Louis, advising business clients, and in 1950 defended members of the Communist Party against diverse criminal charges. Kenneth Royall practiced in Raleigh, representing business interests, until he was activated as a colonel in the JAG Corps. A few months later, he was assigned to defend German saboteurs, and he took their case to civil courts and to the Supreme Court of the United States, in direct defiance of his commander in chief.[10] He also took a stand against Senator McCarthy.[11] What Acheson, Cross, Green, and Royall did in these events was to put their careers at risk to do what they perceived to be the right thing. Other members of that class of 1917 (including my father) performed other, less-noted acts that were public services sometimes rendered at substantial cost to themselves.

No one can say that any of these courageous public acts were a consequence of the teaching of the Bull. But it is possible that they learned in law school to look out for their own moral standards without close guidance from mentors, and gained confidence in their ability to do so. I am sure that many of them practiced law with moral courage, and we can say that the Bull's teaching, so despicable to young Kennedy and others of his generation, had that result as its aim. Maybe it even had some of that effect. I doubt that teachers who would have gratified the young Kennedy with entertaining lectures would have been likely to have done better in training students to stand on their own moral and intellectual feet.

I wonder what the mature Kennedy would propose today in lieu of his utopian proposal of 1983. One of the realities with which he would have to deal is troubling change in that part of the profession advising large corporate enterprises such as Enron. Lawyers in such organizations are increasingly subordinates in hierarchies that are sometimes uncaring.[12]

Whereas members of the class of 1917 were often called by their clients for broad advice, today's partners less frequently have the kind of stable relationship with their clients that results in that kind of consultation. It may well be, for example, that no independent lawyer (i.e., one who had not been subordinated by his or her corporate managers) was ever invited to give advice about the antics of Enron's executives. Even the Bull could not hope to do much about that.

Moreover, the utopian planner today would need to confront the destructive force of law school rankings, which have a paralyzing effect on the freedom of most law schools to do anything that might diminish their relative standings. Virtually every measurement of law schools' employed in rankings counts expenditures, and virtually all available funds must be spent to protect schools' rankings. Also, their shared preoccupation with such matters must reinforce in students a sense that it is affect and not substance that matters.

I have elsewhere proposed my own utopian law school for the twenty-first century.[13] It would have as its aim a result not so very different from Kennedy's "left law school." My proposal requires an elite university with an endowment that its trustees might be willing to invest in the creation of a morally independent legal profession of lawyers unwilling to surrender their autonomy to mindless or greedy hierarchs. My utopian law school would simply forswear tuition, proclaiming that it would conduct the best three-year program it could without charging students for it. Classes would be large, and services other than classroom teaching would be minimal. To assure their moral independence in shaping their careers, students would be enjoined to borrow no money and to live within their current means, however modest those might be. But the university might proclaim that its law school is a contribution to the Republic, much in the tradition envisioned by the eighteenth-century founders of American university legal education[14] and maintained by the University of Michigan in the time of Thomas Cooley.[15] Their graduates would be instructed to repay any indebtedness they felt they owed to the university by serving the public interest as they might best identify that interest.

My Utopia Law School would not do well in the rankings provided by *U.S. News and World Report* because it could not compete in the expenditure of money. Imaginably, it might nevertheless attract adult students who were seriously committed to their own moral values and were willing and able to manage their own intellectual affairs. Their commitments and moral standards might even be reinforced by the moral ambience created by their classmates. The school's graduates might actually prove to have special value to the causes they chose to serve. But even Utopia would not be immune to the charge that it was reproducing hierarchy, because it would hope to shape its students as hierarchs serving benign causes of their choosing.

NOTES

1. This is a comment on DUNCAN KENNEDY, LEGAL EDUCATION AND THE REPRODUCTION OF HIERARCHY: A POLEMIC AGAINST THE SYSTEM (Cambridge, 1983) prepared for inclusion in a republication of that essay by the New York University Press.

2. I have read an account of the Yale Law School of that era written and soon to be published by Laura Kalman. She made helpful comments on an earlier draft of this comment.

3. In 1970, I was assigned to serve as a hearing officer for the University of Michigan Graduate School to consider the cases of students who had disrupted a mathematics class. The leader of the disrupters was a graduate student in chemistry. (I fined him $100; he dropped out rather than pay it.)

4. Letter to R. Rosenwald, May 13, 1927, quoted in, JACK & JACK, MORAL VISION AND PROFESSIONAL DECISIONS 156 (Cambridge UK, 1989).

5. THE BLANK SLATE: THE MODERN DENIAL OF HUMAN NATURE (New York, 2002).

6. All the stories in that celebrated novel were circulating at the Harvard Law School in 1952, when I was a first-year student. It is not unlikely that many of them had gained color from frequent repetition. The novelist used all but one of the stories I heard. The one he did not use was my favorite. It was reported that a student was so agitated after reading the Property examination questions to which he had to respond that he drank his ink. He was taken to a convenient nursing station where the ink could be pumped out of his stomach. As he was returning to consciousness, the Bull entered the nursing station and asked him how he was feeling. "Okay, I guess, Professor Warren." "That's good," the Bull was alleged to have said, "because you have only forty-five minutes to finish the exam."

7. EDWARD H. WARREN, SPARTAN EDUCATION (Boston, 1942).

8. Acheson wrote four volumes of autobiography and he is the subject of five biographies.

9. He argued that lawyers sometimes have a duty to lie in *Ethics of Advocacy,* 4 STAN. L. REV. 3 (1951). A response is Henry Drinker, *Some Remarks on Mr. Curtis,* 4 STAN. L. REV. 349 (1952).

10. Ex parte *Quirin,* 317 U.S. 1 (1942).

11. *American Freedom and the Law: Fighting the Communist Menace,* 40 A.B.A.J. 559 (1953).

12. For comment on that change, see PAUL HASKELL, WHY LAWYERS BE-HAVE AS THEY DO (Boulder, 1998).

13. *On Ranking,* J. LEG. ED. (forthcoming 2003).

14. For a brief account, see Paul D. Carrington, *The Revolutionary Idea of University Legal Education,* 31 WM. & MARY L. REV. 527 (1990).

15. PAUL D. CARRINGTON, STEWARDS OF DEMOCRACY: LAW AS A PUBLIC PROFESSION 25–34 (Boulder, 1999).

The Spiritual Foundation of Attachment to Hierarchy

Peter Gabel

When Duncan Kennedy published *Legal Education and the Reproduction of Hierarchy* in 1983, Ronald Reagan had been in office for three years, and the dominant culture's ultimately (largely) successful war against the 1960s was in full swing. But at that time our fate was not sealed, and in the world of legal education, the Critical Legal Studies (CLS) movement was "hot"—the subject of serious legal symposia in the Stanford and Texas law reviews, a cause for extensive hand-wringing and outrage by icons of the legal establishment, the subject of major (largely denunciatory) articles in the *New Yorker,* the *New Republic,* and national newspapers concerned that the Harvard and Stanford Law Schools in particular were being taken over by radicals. We were also a source of real energy and hope for ourselves—young law professors who had been shaped by the utopian aspirations of the 1960s for a democratic and egalitarian society and who wanted to carry our insights forward toward the transformation of legal education and the whole world—as well as for the generation of law students following us, who could still feel in the air the idealism and basic rightness of that idealism that was pulsing through us and pushing us all forward. Hundreds of people attended our annual conferences that took place at a different leading law school each year; men, women, and increasingly men and women of color engaged in intense intellectual debate during the day and danced late into the night to the Rolling Stones and Aretha Franklin; and weeklong summer camps became exhilarating annual gatherings full of serious study and fun. Although the planning for them may have been in the works in some Washington think tanks, the Federalist Societies had not yet taken their place as campus institutions—societies that were eventually publicly blessed and thanked by Ronald Reagan himself, toward the end of his second term, for having decisively defeated the plague to our national well-being known as Critical Legal Studies.

Duncan's "little red book" was thus flung into a historical moment ripe with hope, and yet with storm clouds on the horizon that would eventually overwhelm us. Those storm clouds were not by any means exclusively the creation of our opponents—they were in significant part the result of the limitations of our own vision and of the movements of the '60s themselves, including our own. In my opinion, some of those limitations are reflected in Duncan's book, and I will address them momentarily. But first I want to state what is brilliant and important about the book, and how the ideas in it accurately express the relationship between the revelations unveiled by the movements of the '60s and the critique of legal education as one embodiment of the reproduction of hierarchy that, to use Duncan's word, "maims" all of us by depriving us of our capacity for freedom and collective self-determination—as well as (and this prefigures my critique of the book) our spiritual capacity to become fully present to ourselves and to each other in relations of loving human connection and mutual recognition.

When I say that Duncan published his book in the midst of a war waged by the dominant culture against the movements of the '60s, what I mean by "war" is not primarily a struggle over power over who will run the economic system or the institutions of American society but a war over the nature of consciousness, and the nature of reality itself. The '60s was fundamentally not a movement for reform or revolution according to the inherited meaning of those words, as if what the world needed was a reordering of the external relationships of reality to make economic and political "systems" more equal, or to overthrow the power of the ruling class and replace it with some kind of externally pictured mass democracy, or anything of that kind. The movement was rather a movement of desire, of aspiration, an opening up of closed space that allowed millions of people to come to see and feel something invisible—namely, the artificiality and even unreality of the inherited world and the possibility of a better, more humane, and more real one.

Many, many forces contributed to this opening up of desire, among them the civil rights movement, Elvis, the Beat Poets, the evocative lyricism of JFK, the insufferable lack of oxygen in the atmosphere of the post–World War II kitchen culture of the 1950s. But the main factor was the Vietnam War and the growing awareness that dawned on millions of young people in particular that something insane was taking place, and it was taking place not because the war was in the economic interests of General Motors but because in some sense the whole world was out of its mind, out of touch with Being itself, living out scripts that rationalized the mass murder of millions of human beings.

There is an album from that period by a rock group called the Electric Flag that illustrates what I mean by this. The opening song on the album begins with then-president Lyndon Johnson saying in the southern drawl that we heard every night on the news, "My Fellow Americans . . . ," followed by a few words, and then a mass of people bursting into laughter. The point was that out of the passive confusion that characterized the initial years of ambivalence toward the war, and out of the contradiction that the draft was posing for all of us of whether we were going to . . . die . . . because it was our "role" to do so, and out of countless televised images of human suffering and death that acquired a surreal character as all of us faced with this contradiction gradually grasped that real people, and not televised images, were dying without any plausible narrative intelligibility (without any story we could tell ourselves of why this made sense)—out of all this came the genuine insight that Lyndon Johnson was in some way merely playing the role of "president" and that things were happening, real events were occurring, that were the outcome of large masses of people all playing one role or another in the reproduction of a society that was unable to stop this war precisely because they were entrapped in these roles.

I say that this insight was an expression of the opening up of desire because it emerged through a liberating process of *mutual* discovery, in which each of us was suddenly brought into a palpably more authentic contact with others through a dawning "shock of recognition." Out of the drifty isolation of our passive conditioning, in which we were simply to play out the passive roles assigned to us by accident of birth and the cultural predestinations that followed from our class, race, gender, and a multitude of other social attributes, we suddenly felt galvanized into a movement of more connected and more real human beings who could, must, actively shape a more authentic destiny for ourselves and a more just and loving world. Through this phenomenal ricochet of mutual recognition that spread rapidly across the entire face of the earth, what had been invisible became visible, and a kind of authentic, elevating love and joy spread across the psycho-spiritual energy field that was social existence itself.

That turning of the spirit outward toward the other is the true meaning of the word *movement,* since, of course, nobody physically moves anywhere except during demonstrations or when dancing to music.

But this process of revelation did not instantly change the inherited world and its institutions, values, loyalties, and distributions of power and wealth. On the contrary, although we eventually stopped the war, the patterns of social identity that shaped American institutions kept grinding along, and the farther one was from the liberating experience of the movement, the more one resisted and was even enraged by the movement's challenge to the legitimacy of everything that one's conditioning had led one to feel was the basis of one's very social existence and connection to others. Furthermore, the conflict about the very nature of social reality existed within the heart of everyone who was "in" the movement as well as those outside it—we ourselves were threatened by our opposition to the parents who had raised us and whose love and values and ways of life we had internalized, and in any case, we had no idea how to create our own new world, whole cloth, out of nothing but a powerful, blinding insight, when the weight of history had produced the institutions and the means of material subsistence that were the only ways of life that were "really there" in front of us. Thus the "war" that the movement(s) of the 1960s sparked in the culture was a war between two consciousnesses of reality existing not "between" different collections of individuals but side by side within the whole of social consciousness that was still, for the most part (for there were many, many radical experiments that tried to start over from scratch), the inherited world suffused with the norms, ideas, and values of prior generations. Thus the origin of the German radical Rudi Dutschke's famous injunction to all of us who became activists determined to change the world in accordance with our newfound insights: "We've had the '60s. Now for the long march through the institutions."

Legal Education and the Reproduction of Hierarchy is an expression of one ingenious mind's attempt to bring what was authentic in our awareness to an unveiling of the encrusted and "maiming" patterns of passive alienation in one of the institutions that *as a totality* generated the Vietnam War (fifty-five thousand Americans, two million Asians dead, for "nothing") and that was trying to continue on indefinitely reproducing this social alienation in future generations. Duncan's book is not mainly about law school but about the reproduction of hierarchy within the society as a whole, in a way that actually constitutes the society by recruiting each new generation to become passive actors, role-players, in relationship to a self-legitimating set of ideas and patterns of deference and authority. It is about law school only in the sense that it is a detailed phenomenological description of one particular such institution that Duncan himself is immersed in, and in the sense that his "theory" is precisely that it is through telling the story of *his* world, in enough detail to make it uncontrovertibly recognizable to the reader, that one can "recognize" the nature of society as a whole as a consciousness war more or less corresponding to the big war of the '60s I've just described in larger societal terms. In other words, it is about law school in the very specific sense that law school is training for hierarchy generally, *and* that law school is one very important hierarchy itself, insofar as its training has as its specific aim teaching the "legitimating ideology" that serves to legitimate all the others. This last point is, in fact, hardly touched on in this book—it appears only in the description of the role of the curriculum in transmitting the presupposed legitimacy of the basic rules of the "private" capitalist marketplace in contracts, torts, and property during the first year and the center-left consensus of modest reforms of capitalism institutionalized in the New Deal during the second year—but it is a major theme of the rest of most Critical Legal Studies writing, and its minor presence here is an important bridge to that writing. The vast majority of the book in the first six descriptive chapters is devoted to the first main idea of revealing, mainly through the use of concrete, expressive examples, how the hierarchy reproduces itself as an alienation factory, as a process of bondage.

To understand the book and its relationship to the consciousness-war theory of our society that I am claiming it is an expression of, it is important to grasp that the book was written *against* the received views of the Left about the role of law and legal education in maintaining the existing order of things. In 1983, the received view, prevalent within the National Lawyers Guild and the Left in general, was either that law is an instrument of the ruling class "used" by those in power to maintain their class superiority in relation to an economic system that is the true locus of social struggle, or that law is a potential tool of gradual change through statutory or common-law liberal reforms that will give space to the oppressed to fight for more fundamental change. Duncan spells out his critique of both positions in the book itself, mainly by emphasizing, for example, that the market and the state are now so interpenetrated that it is meaningless to say one is "more fundamental" than the other, or that the idea that today's "proletariat" of the marginalized poor (he names welfare mothers, illegal immigrants, and the homeless) is going to lead the revolution is just implausible, or that the reform strategy just can't work because external modifications of the System remain encapsulated within the internal re-production of hierarchical patterning that *is* the system. And he shows how both theories serve as rationalizations that actually disempower law students from engaging in struggle right now to transform law schools as part of the anarcho-syndicalist, workplace-by-workplace organizing that the book advocates as the cell-by-cell way to actually change the world.

But through the consciousness-war lens of the historical period that I am emphasizing, the most important error in the received left views of law was precisely that they picture law and legal education as "tools" of domi-nation within an "entity" called society that actually does not exist—be-cause what *does* exist is the consciousness war between authenticity and alienation that is masked and denied precisely by "the reproduction of hi-erarchy" that keeps spreading itself across the face of the networks of human interaction we call society. Duncan is not denying the existence or importance of economic inequality and injustice or of other forms of in-equality and injustice that CLS, as one incarnation of the Left, was/is fight-ing against. But he is writing a work of expressive revelation that makes a demand on the reader to recognize that the source of the problem is not "out there" but right in front of him or her, a condition of existential servitude to a great nothing (the hierarchy with no heart or center to it) masked by a kind of universal fealty that is just self-deception and "false consciousness." Thus the strategy in the last chapters of the book calls not for changing "society," as if there were some External Thing outside of us that we had to somehow manipulate into democracy and egalitarianism and, as lawyers (law professors, law students), "use" law as a "tool" to do so, but rather for cellular organizing to resist the pain right now of having one's existence as a free being "maimed" by a distortion of social con-sciousness that is always occurring where we are, right now. Within this ef-fort, law is not a "tool" but a part of the consciousness, encoding values le-gitimating hierarchy that are masked by claims to neutrality and mere craft ("legal reasoning") that can and should be exposed and contested just as the institution, law school, that teaches that law should be.

What is ingenious about the book is not the correctness of this point of view stated abstractly, but the revelatory power of the description of law school itself. Every detail of life in law school—from the way the interac-tion of the hard case and the soft case seduces the student into accepting, and the way each is taught draws the student into believing in, the power of legal as opposed to "nonlegal" reasoning; to the way that fatuous attacks on law professors in the law school student paper actually help constitute the pedestal on which the very meanest of professors must be located (as does the mercy dispensed by these very professors: "his Clark is worse than his Byse"); to the way that the tiniest of gestures serve as modeling displays, made coercive by the fact that everyone watching everyone else follows them (the students seeing "'secretaries' treating 'professors' with elaborate deference, as though her time and her dignity meant nothing and his everything, even when he is not her boss," and that humane relations between them, when they occur, "are a matter of the superior's grace, rather than of humane need and social justice"); to the role of law review ("An instant ('the lightning of grades') converts jerks into statesmen; honored spokespeople retire to the margins, shamed"); to the microdetails of social coercion students learn to impose on themselves that both reinforce and erase class and race hierarchies ("Lower-middle class students learn not to wear an undershirt that shows, and that certain patterns and fabrics in clothes will stigmatize them no matter what their grades," while "Black students learn . . . that their very presence means affirmative action, unless it means 'he would have made it even without affirmative action'") is subjected to Duncan's X-ray vision and made transparent as a more or less unified way of life that *seems* impossible to escape from and serves as training for the later hierarchies of the Bar, whose saints come marching in, as Duncan also describes, beginning with the interview process of the second year and the fancy hotels you will be invited to fly out to stay in, to the denial of humiliation that is manifested in the "ha, ha" mass posting of one's rejection letters in the dorms, and so on right up through one's poignant death (this part is not in the book but is implied by it), when one may realize for the first time that one has lived a life imprisoned in masks that turned into a false self, a life without freedom, authentic personal dignity, and the integrity of self-determination.

As a way of showing both the strengths and limitations of the book as I see it, and of establishing the relationship of the book to the work of Critical Legal Studies as a whole, let me again call Duncan's method "expressive revelation" and separate this method into two consciousnesses: Duncan's own consciousness, which I call the *seeing* consciousness, and the consciousness that he is attempting to expressively reveal or unveil, which I call the *seen* consciousness, that of the role-player caught up in the drama of the reproduction of law school hierarchy. In my view, the seeing consciousness, as it is manifested in all the book's examples of training for hierarchy, is brilliantly insightful and is aligned with what I earlier described as the liberating consciousness of the movements of the '60s. The seeing consciousness purports to be free and is making a powerful appeal to the seeing consciousness in the reader to identify with this freedom through the unveiling of the "false consciousness" of the seen consciousness. And it proposes concrete strategies (cell-by-cell organizing, the Left Study Group) where possibilities of resistance to the enveloping power of the seen consciousness can be "cracked open," resisted, and effectively contested.

So far, so good.

But the problem, as I see it, comes with the seen consciousness, for a central characteristic of the seen consciousness is that it *does not wish to be seen.* Indeed, the entire point of the book is to show that this consciousness comes into being through an elaborate process of "imprisonment," in which each act of modeling deference to hierarchy—together producing a kind of unified ubiquity of social interactions, as well as mystifying ideas that cement this hierarchy in the group's self-reflection—is designed both to keep reproducing the hierarchy and to prevent this intention from becoming visible. As Duncan puts it, what is initially a mask becomes the self. His point is precisely that the reproduction of hierarchy is elaborated through what I would call a "circle of collective denial," or through what he on several occasions calls a denial of "false consciousness" that is coercively made unaware of its own falseness. This aspect of what I am calling the seen consciousness provides the link between the unveiling insight of the movements of the '60s—its insight into the unreality of a society of people playing roles that are mistaken for "who we really are"—and Duncan's own insights into legal education as one important arena where this process takes place and reproduces itself, like an amoeba.

The reason that this aspect of the seen consciousness is a problem is that the book assumes that the seen consciousness can be resisted and eventually undone by a spreading of the seeing consciousness's discovery of its own freedom—through revealing the seen consciousness for what it is and engaging in forms of political organizing that oppose the hierarchy's false claims in the name of freedom and true collective self-determination. In my view, however, this contradicts the very *social* nature of the reproduction of hierarchy, in which people gain recognition and their personal identity as social beings connected to others by accommodating to the world of others that surrounds them. Indeed, the only plausible explanation for why law students don't spontaneously resist and reject their assimilation to a hierarchy that "maims" them and deprives them of their authentic selfhood is that the reproduction of hierarchy is the reproduction of our own social alienation, to which, absent some liberating social movement that frees us for a more authentic form of social connection, we have no choice but to succumb. To apply this very insight to the revelatory power of the seeing consciousness, Duncan's own capacity to see through and express the alienated character of legal education and the reproduction of hierarchy generally is not the result of the freedom and insight of a singular individual (here, Duncan himself) but rather the expression of the insight of an era that is itself an expression of an inherently *social* movement of inherently social beings liberated (only partially, alas) from their social alienation and inherited conditioning by the affirming gaze of the Other, with each serving as the Other for the Other. Just as the coercive denial spread throughout the law school hierarchy is made coercive by making accommodation serve as a condition of social membership and identity, so also the capacity for freedom from the hierarchy—the capacity even to see it as social alienation—requires the Other: others who form the more real and more present and more free and more authentically connected consciousness of the movement.

The limitation of Duncan's book is that it does not, in my opinion, accurately analyze the cause of the very "sickness" he describes, a limitation that links the book to what became the dominant point of view in Critical Legal Studies and that must be transcended if we are to pick up where we left off. The work of CLS was always divided into two main strands, what might be called the critique of alienation, on the one hand, and the neolegal realist/deconstruction critique, which became known as the "indeterminacy" critique, on the other. In part because of the influence of virtually all of Duncan's other writings about law, the indeterminacy critique became the dominant one within CLS and was devoted almost exclusively to demonstrating, in a myriad of specific instances—in hundreds of articles—what is merely alluded to in the first chapter of *Legal Education and the Reproduction of Hierarchy*: namely, that all legal reasoning, as well as justifications for the alleged legitimacy of legal reasoning (e.g., the work of Ronald Dworkin), can be shown to be sufficiently vague, circular, self-contradictory, or manipulable so as to not provide any plausible justification claiming to legitimately dictate the outcomes of cases. Although in its phenomenological or descriptive aspect *Legal Education and the Reproduction of Hierarchy* is mainly Duncan's best published description of the alienation critique, in its separation of the seeing consciousness and the seen consciousness the book is also consistent with the indeterminacy critique.

For the indeterminacy critique is fundamentally not a critique that uses the social-phenomenological method of "expressive revelation" to unveil the alienated character of legal thought and culture but rather what I would call a neoformalist analytical mode of critique that seeks to affirm the freedom of the reader from the alleged determinacy of legal doctrine and justifications for doctrine. In this respect, the indeterminacy critique spilled into and joined forces with poststructuralism, identity politics, and deconstruction, which more or less took over CLS and the academic Left as a whole with the collapse of socialism and Marxist criticism.

The problem with the indeterminacy critique is that it wants to argue for democracy and egalitarianism by showing that we are all free from any purported state of bondage to legal rules and the political justifications for them, but it leaves us each alone in our freedom—it does not want to come to grips with the social nature of the alienation critique, which accounts for the illusion of bondage by its recognition that the seen consciousness clings to the determinacy and the purported legitimacy of law and legal institutions *because it does not wish to become conscious of itself.* Whether or not it's a denial of false consciousness, people are just not going to give up their attachment to the alienated networks of passive role-performances, or their belief in the legitimacy of legal reasoning and legal education, if maintaining their allegiance to these modes of alienation is their only apparent source of social identity and self-worth as inherently social beings, and bowing to this alienation is even the seemingly necessary condition of group membership. The relationship of Duncan's book to the indeterminacy critique in CLS scholarship is that both covertly assume that people will *want* to reclaim their freedom, from hierarchy as well as from the supposed objectivity that rationalizes the legitimacy of legal reasoning, if their freedom from the "false necessity" of following the rules can be shown to them (in the case of hierarchy, through this particular book's method of demystifying "expressive revelation"; in the case of legal reasoning, by the analytical deconstruction of the purported rationality of the thought process). But this is not the case if freedom's just another word for nothing left to lose, and if unfreedom is the only source of fulfilling the longing for mutual recognition and social connection that inheres in the nature of social existence itself.

It was Martin Luther King Jr. who most fully grasped this truth in relation to law when he defined justice as "Love correcting that which revolts against love." The point of this idea in relation to the reproduction of hierarchy is that the "sickness" of the "maiming" hierarchies of legal education that Duncan so brilliantly describes is a spiritual sickness that must be healed by new methods of educating lawyers that bind them to the moral ideal of creating a loving and caring society. Like Duncan's book itself, the '60s provided my generation with a glimpse of King's insight, a glimpse of our essential possibility for authentic and loving connection that could transcend the spiritual distortion of our forced allegiance to the legacy of social alienation that we inherited from prior generations and that were indeed, as Duncan says, a form of collective denial, of "false consciousness." But the glimpse turned out to be too brief and too frightening in its very radicalism to allow us to develop the way out of the claim that our prior conditioning made upon our loyalties; and within both CLS and the '60s themselves, we were not yet able to link the experience of the possibility of liberation-through-each-other with what many spiritual traditions call The Way, the details of the spiritual strategy to successfully transform our servitude to hierarchy into an authentic, beloved community.

What would this mean in relation to the transformation of legal education in a more "just" direction, within the meaning of King's definition? Paradoxically, I am in substantial agreement with a core element of the last chapters on strategy in *Legal Education and the Reproduction of Hierarchy*—the vision of an existential, cell-by-cell transformation of the whole in which concrete groups of students, teachers, and lawyers see the hierarchies before them as an unnecessary network of mutually legitimating denial of authentic human longing that rationalizes alienation, domination, and even cruelty and that must be overcome piecemeal, rather than, say, by seizing control of the state or the means of production or any of the other "totalizing" strategies that in 1983 were part of the dominant left fantasy about replacing the current order of things. I also think there is some appropriate and limited value to the indeterminacy critique of legal reasoning as an intellectually helpful part of this process, in showing that no political or legal *concept*, no matter how lofty (liberty, equality, democracy), can be shown to *entail* a particular result, which is to say, to entail the realization of the ideal claimed by that concept. As one moment of the spiritual awakening that leads our students and ourselves to move toward correcting that which revolts against Love, it is helpful to see that this has nothing to do with the concept of love, which is of course indeterminate in what it entails, but rather with the undistorting, the healing, and the re-sacralization of our experience of one another as social beings whom we can come to recognize as the source of each other's completion.

But to "correct," in King's sense, what should have been the main theme of CLS (that the legal system legitimates social alienation) and what is the main accomplishment of Duncan's book as a critique of legal education as an instance of reproducing social alienation, this path of cell-by-cell transformation must be reunderstood as a morally compelling, spiritual activity rather than merely an intellectual/political revolt of free individuals against a surrounding false consciousness. The work of transformation must offer those who engage in it the kind of social healing and legal wisdom that is capable of healing the underlying motivation for the maiming collective *denial* upon which the book places so much emphasis, a denial that otherwise will not be capable of becoming conscious of itself by overcoming the counterinfluence of the processes of social coercion that institutionalize that denial and keep reproducing it, as they have successfully continued to do from 1983 until today.

The Project for Integrating Spirituality, Law and Politics, of which I am a member, is a group of lawyers, law teachers, and law students who are trying to do precisely this: to engage in the piecemeal spiritual disalienation and transformation of the legal profession, of which legal education is a very important part. I also work in one cell of legal education, New College of California's public-interest law school, and in a cell within that cell, the first-year course in Contracts that I have taught for almost thirty years.

In that cell within a cell within a cell, every year I teach the case of *O'Neal v. Colton School Board of the State of Washington.* Mr. O'Neal was a longtime schoolteacher in Colton High School who had developed diabetes and found, late one spring, that he could no longer read well enough to see his students' papers, to read either their writing or the board in his classroom. During the summer following the end of that school year, he reluctantly decided that he had no choice worthy of his students and his school but to inform the School Board that he could not return the next year, although he was "under contract" to do so. The School Board shocked Mr. O'Neal by replying that he had no justification for "refusing to perform" and rejected his attempted resignation, denying him in the process his request for his accumulated twenty-seven and a half sick days. The legal issue presented to the students by the casebook, and the case itself, is whether Mr. O'Neal was excused from "performing" under the doctrine of impossibility of performance.

It is possible to teach this case in many ways. One is to ask a student from a position of superior knowledge, backed by the threat of humiliation and nonrecognition of the student's legal talent, a question designed to test the student's capacity to see that Mr. O'Neal should have foreseen the risk of his disabling illness prior to entering his contract, and that to excuse him under these circumstances would both undermine personal responsibility for assumed risks and bring inefficiency and instability into market transactions where no transaction costs are present that might justify governmental interference in the market (a law-and-economics method of conditioning students to embrace the legitimacy of competitive individualism and a materialist conception of value popular today, although largely unheard of in 1983). Another, certainly more common approach would be to use the same interpersonal methods to compare Mr. O'Neal's resignation to, say, a deep-sea diver's refusal to go through with an agreement to dive for valuable pearls for fear of being attacked by sharks, an exercise in distinguishing cases involving foreseeable risks that eliminates the fancy philosophy (if law-and-economics can be considered such) and reduces legal reasoning to more of a trade involving cleverness but transmitting the same values to students. Still a third, more liberal approach would be to adopt the same superior stance as the teacher but treat *O'Neal v. Colton* as just an easy case to get across the rule that serious illness forms the basis for a valid impossibility defense in employment cases, but to focus on the Court's formalistic refusal to allow him the sick days, which the Court says fell through because accumulated sick days must be claimed before the end of one's employment, and the contract was terminated at the moment of impossibility when the diabetes disabled Mr. O'Neal from performing. Even more "political" would be an effort to bring out the labor movement's long struggle to win the granting of accumulated sick days at all for workers in a market characterized by inequality of wealth and power and the injustice of the opinion's formalism in light of the length of Mr. O'Neal's employment.

Personally, in my cell, I have used all the foregoing methods, although to the extent that I employ the "Socratic" posture in my egalitarian school, I do it playfully, to remove the (in my opinion) absurd implication that it is humiliating not to know the fancy (1) or clever (2) or historically informed (3) answer. And I explicitly bring out at the end of this portion of the discussion what the rule is in employment cases.

But then I ask a question that addresses what I honestly, deeply feel about Mr. O'Neal as I have thought about him and his family over the years. I ask a student how a local community ought to respond with justice to a long time, perhaps venerated high school teacher who has taught most, if not all, the children in the town of Colton, many of whom are now grown, many of whom now have children of their own who benefited from Mr. O'Neal's teaching. Under all the traditional approaches to teaching the case described above, the very best treatment Mr. O'Neal receives means going home alone with a little money to at most his wife and children, if he has a wife and children, to rattle around in retirement half-blind until he dies. Might it be our *legal* obligation—that is, the legal obligation of the School Board as the embodiment of the community—to keep him on as an elder, to make sure he is venerated and appreciated and taken care of and even given an active mentoring role in the school that doesn't require the eyesight acuity of everyday teaching? Mightn't this elevate the later years of Mr. O'Neal's life, give great pleasure to his former students, bring a greater sense of community to the high school as a whole, and strengthen the high school's ties to the rest of the town?

In my view, it is this sort of approach, writ large and reimagined toward transforming the whole moral and spiritual nature of the curriculum, as well as informing the teaching of the nature of the social interventions one might consider trying to make as a lawyer in the school's clinics and later as a lawyer in practice, that undermines the reproduction of hierarchy and carries forward the promise of Critical Legal Studies. The reason is that this approach touches on the longing for a beloved community, and of law as a path to the creation of such a community, that exists in each of us—indeed, even consciously in virtually all law students on the first day of law school, before they are conditioned to become clever, cynical arguers for the materialist self-interest of clients at the expense of their brothers and sisters. Or to put it differently, in my view there is no "opposite" of the reproduction of social alienation and hierarchy except for the *experience* of love and community, and then the reproduction of the experience until it becomes confident of itself. As Duncan's dear and lifelong friend, I actually am confident that this is the inspiration behind his "polemic against the system"—his brilliant and, at the time of publication, daring little red book.

Power and Resistance in
Contemporary Legal Education

Angela Harris and Donna Maeda

What struck us first upon reading Duncan Kennedy's polemic twenty years later was, sadly, how fresh it is. The relations of power in the ordinary law school and those between the ordinary law school and the world of practice—described and decried by Kennedy as "hierarchy"—are more or less the same. With the exception of the clinical programs that increasingly round out the average curriculum (programs that have largely failed to have the transformative effect on the institution that Kennedy hoped for), not much has changed in the process or substance of legal education since he wrote. Indeed, not much has changed in legal education since Christopher Columbus Langdell and Charles Eliot first popularized Langdell's curriculum at Harvard Law School at the beginning of the twentieth century.[1] Nor has the potential of using the law to "do well by doing good" changed since Kennedy wrote, except for the worse: when Kennedy wrote, it was still possible to graduate from law school, take a job in legal services, and make a pretty good living. It is no longer so today.[2]

Kennedy's polemic, then, remains a useful field guide for understanding the political economy of legal education. Nevertheless, it may be interesting to place its publication in some historical context. *Legal Education and the Reproduction of Hierarchy* came out roughly fifteen years after the Third World Liberation Strike of 1968–69 at San Francisco State, Berkeley, and other campuses pushed university administrations around the country to institute Black Studies, Chicano Studies, Asian Studies, and Native American Studies programs and to develop "theme houses" and other race- and ethnicity-centered organizations and programs.[3] The students who demanded these programs saw the university as a base from which to work for political change in racialized communities, as well as a place where cultural assimilation could be resisted in the hope of strengthening racialized consciousness and pride. Their vision was intellectual as well as political and social: the founders of the Ethnic Studies programs argued that Americans in general were ignorant of their own history, and that the study of the traditional disciplines was incomplete without recognition of the United States' complex history of racial subjugation.

Just over ten years after *Legal Education and the Reproduction of Hierarchy* came out, the National History Standards Project—composed of a consortium of nine educational organizations, backed by political leaders in the Bush I administration, and funded by agencies such as the National Endowment for the Humanities—would issue a set of national standards for the teaching of history that instantly served as a flashpoint for ideological attack.[4] An assemblage of public figures ranging from Lynne Cheney, head of the National Endowment for the Humanities, to conservative commentator Rush Limbaugh would assail the integrity of the standards and their creators. On the floor of the U.S. Senate, Senator Slade Gorton of Washington denounced the standards as an "ideologically driven anti-West monument to politically correct caricature," designed "to destroy our Nation's mystic chords of memory."[5] By a vote of ninety-nine to one, the Senate recommended rejection of the standards, a move that had more symbolic than instrumental effect. The flap enacted in miniature the drama of the 1990s "culture wars," which, as Gary Nash, Charlotte Crabtree, and Ross Dunn put it, pitted "militant monoculturalists of the Right," who demanded that history promote "Ozzie and Harriet patriotism and exclusive celebration of the Western tradition," against "militant multiculturalists . . . [who had] romanticized the history of their particular group or region out of all recognition, and stigmatized Western civilization as the world's oldest evil empire."[6]

We write as a faculty member and a student at Boalt Hall, School of Law at the University of California–Berkeley, an academic institution with a long and vibrant history of left student protest. Here at Berkeley (but not only here), thirty-five years of anti-racist campus politics have helped diversify the faculty and the student body. Although the desegregation of law school faculties has predictably been slower and more uneven than the desegregation of student bodies—and although both trends are threatened by backlash and economic hard times at the state and local levels—this demographic shift has in the meantime increased racial, ethnic, cultural, and gender diversity in legal education.

As the story of the culture wars suggests, the sometimes violent and hard-fought project of anti-subordination struggle on campus and off has had an intellectual effect as well. Students entering law school with liberal educations now are increasingly likely to have read not only Karl Marx but also Michel Foucault, Gayatri Chakravorti Spivak, and Homi Bhabha. A tide of "theory" has swept the humanities and, to a lesser extent, the social sciences. It has even infiltrated the legal academy, as reflected not only in Kennedy's own work as a founder of Critical Legal Studies but also in the large and increasingly sophisticated literatures of critical race theory and Latino/a critical theory, feminist legal theory, and queer theory.

These new political and intellectual resources, and the new faces in legal education that these resources reflect, make possible a different student reaction to the reproduction of legal hierarchy. Kennedy's analysis seems aimed at the student with no previous experience of organizing resistance and no resources (other than liberal or Marxist ideology) for understanding structures of power: it offers aid and comfort to the student who has come to law school to confront these structures for the first time and has found himself or herself overwhelmed. In 2003, law school is more likely than before to be experienced by students for whom a sense of institutional alienation and the experience of organizing is not new, and for whom the law is neither the first nor the primary site at which hierarchy is reproduced or undermined.

This alternative perspective or "stance" does not solve the dilemmas of law and social change; nor do most students arrive at law school with their consciousnesses already raised. Nevertheless, the intellectual and political resources of such students do make possible a practice of solidarity and collective struggle that can take students beyond the law school study group that Kennedy identifies as the first, baby step toward resistance and into the hard work of coalition politics that characterizes contemporary movements for racial justice both inside and outside the academy.

I.

Kennedy describes two attitudes toward the law available to the left law student of 1983. First, there is what we might call the "liberal" approach:

students come to law school because they believe that the American legal system is a force for justice; as Kennedy puts it, "with a deep belief that in its essence law is a progressive force, however much it may be distorted by the actual arrangements of capitalism" (17). The second stance Kennedy describes—call it the "radical" view—is that the law is corrupt and primarily serves the interests of elites, but that it is possible for the superbly trained and dedicated lawyer, at least sometimes, to turn it against itself. As Kennedy describes this view, "law is a tool of established interests, . . . it is in essence superstructural, but . . . it is a tool a coldly effective professional can sometimes turn against the dominators" (17).

In Kennedy's polemic, these two positions exhaust the possibilities for the left law student. They are still common today. Some version of the liberal narrative remains the most popular story told by left law school applicants in their "personal statements." A stunningly large proportion of Boalt Hall applicants describe in these statements an encounter with a person or persons less privileged than themselves (often during their junior year abroad), through which they realized the existence of structural injustice, recognized that this injustice has a legal dimension, and became convinced that legal training would give them the power to right the wrong. Some version of the radical position, though not so likely to surface in application materials, is still articulated by many students as well. For instance, young graduates who become public defenders privately describe a practice world of conflicting ideologies. Their senior colleagues hold the liberal belief that "the system" works and that their own work plays a critical role in protecting everyone's rights. The younger generation, however, is much more cynical about the American criminal justice system, and at the same time more comfortable with and committed to the actual people they represent. They tend to see the criminal justice system as simply a tool of the elite for subordinating the largely black and brown masses of the poor. Their personal vocation is not to uphold the system but to do what they can for its victims.

We also see, however, a third left stance toward legal education and legal practice that has become visible since Kennedy wrote his piece. Sometimes students come to law school with this stance; other times they struggle toward it in the process of discovering, and resisting, the hierarchies that Kennedy so vividly describes. This third stance shares with the radical view the belief that the law is not neutral, but it abandons the view that the law is the sole site of subordination, and the corresponding view that the role of the radical lawyer is somehow uniquely heroic.

In the world of the academy, this stance is associated with critical theory and "outsider jurisprudence." In the practice world, it is vividly present in the environmental justice movement and more generally in what Gerald Lopez calls "rebellious lawyering." In this essay, we name it *progressive*. The idea is that law, because of its structural biases toward the powerful and because it can be manipulated by the powerful, is a dangerous tool. Yet transformations can and do occur: people engaged in legal struggle can suddenly become aware of capacities they did not know they had, can find solidarity in collective action, and can, sometimes, make that action effective despite the desires of the ostensibly more powerful. This transformation has come to be called "empowerment," and though the word has been overused, it describes something real. Law cannot make empowerment happen; lawyers and legal action can, in fact, foster disempowerment. But the corollary is that if lawyers and the law are not necessarily the most important site of resistance, then transformation can occur despite the continued reproduction of legal hierarchy.

The progressive stance is associated with the emergence of post-Marxist theories of power and the wave of "theory" that swept American campuses in the 1980s and 1990s. Kennedy's polemic was written just as Critical Legal Studies (CLS) was coming into being, and it reflects his intellectual struggle with the "vulgar Marxist" view of power that CLS ultimately transcended. Kennedy explicitly rejects the base/superstructure metaphor of power relations, in which social action at a key point (by the proletariat, for example) can topple the entire edifice and bring about the revolution. Indeed, Kennedy anticipates the thinking of post-Marxists like Etienne Balibar and poststructuralists like Michel Foucault when, for example, he asserts, "What has happened is a simultaneous blurring of lines between classes and institutions that were once distinct (at least in theory) and a diffusion of social power through the hierarchy that has made it, paradoxically, at once more stable and more vulnerable" (106), and suggests that because power is everywhere, resistance is potentially everywhere as well ("it is not only possible but also meaningful to resist anywhere and at any time" [114]).

Yet Kennedy's polemic also does not quite escape the Marxist rhetoric that it resists. His assertion that there is a single, unified "total hierarchical structure" that is "diamond shaped" (101) remains caught in the metaphor of power-as-a-container that Foucault will complicate. Kennedy also is indebted to Marxist rhetoric and the container metaphor for his characterization of this structure as composed of "corporate cells, each of which includes people from different strata doing different tasks," and each of which "roughly mirrors the internal hierarchical arrangement of all the others" (101). Critical views of power have since abandoned the container metaphor and its implication that power is solely repressive. In critical race feminist accounts of power, for example, power is conceived of as a web of interlocking strands.[7] Moreover, in these post-Marxist accounts, power is not only repressive but productive: it does not simply place people in hierarchies but also produces the subject.[8]

Kennedy's analysis differs the most from the stance we call progressive, however, in the way it discusses legal hierarchy in isolation, disconnected except at the most general level from other forms of subordination. The absence of any account of other experiences of resistance—for example, resistance to racism, sexism, homophobia—suggests that his imaginary reader is a student who lacks any such experiences.[9] By considering law students *only* as students, Kennedy does not address those students who experience legal education as one small aspect of a larger project of collective resistance.

From the progressive perspective, state power and the law are indispensable yet not the sole sites for political struggle: neither the hero of the piece, as in liberal views, nor the villain, as in radical views. Instead, the forms of outsider theory and outsider jurisprudence that are rooted in the experiences of subordinated communities walk a tricky line between cynicism and hope, between engagement in legal reform and condemnation of its ability to coopt struggle.[10]

This stance of believing and not believing, of making something out of nothing, of using state power while distrusting the state, is reflected not only in the women's movement, the civil rights movement, and the grassroots movements of gay, lesbian, bisexual, and transgendered people. It is also reflected in the practices of lawyers who serve and have learned from these movements. For instance, about a decade after Kennedy wrote his polemic, Luke Cole (who was Kennedy's student at Harvard Law School) wrote an essay in which he identified three questions to ask of models of environmental advocacy: "Will it educate?; Will it build the movement?; and Will it address the root of the problem or merely a symptom?"[11] Cole was writing from his experience as a lawyer for the environmental justice movement, a movement led by women and people of color to resist the environmental degradation of poor and minority communities.[12] Cole's suggestion was that communities facing environmental racism would do best not to seek leadership from professionals, nor even to seek participation in environmental decision making through traditional channels, but rather to recognize that traditional decision-making procedures are designed to keep disempowered people disempowered. For Cole, the best model for advocacy is what he calls the "power model":

> The power model is more concerned with building viable community organizations than with winning any particular . . . battle. The model recognizes that communities must take ownership of the struggle "and ultimately their own communities." Redlining, racism, unemployment, and crime are long-term problems for low-income communities that long outlive fights over particular facilities. Ideally, environmental justice strategies that build local power will have an impact on these long-term problems. Many community organizations created during the heat of local environmental fights have become creative, contributing community forces for social and economic justice.[13]

Environmental justice activists recognize that the law is not a neutral arbiter of conflicts. Rather, "[a]dherents of the power model believe that the system is stacked and that no amount of participation by itself will change the relations of power that give rise to environmental degradation."[14] Yet these activists do not see the only alternative as "using the law against itself." As Cole puts it:

> The power model teaches its adherents to distrust the system, while also teaching them how to use that system. The power model focuses on educating community residents to take power for themselves. This power over their own lives, or self-determination, is a central part of environmental justice. Peggy Shepard, a founder of West Harlem Environmental Action, asserts that "[s]elf-determination is a crucial aspect of improving the quality of life in many communities of color." In its ideal form, the power model teaches communities to take control of their own environments.[15]

Lawyers are not irrelevant to the environmental justice movement, but neither are they central. Lawyering for environmental justice under the power model thus becomes a form of rebellious lawyering,[16] lawyering that takes its cue from the political communities it serves.

II.

Students currently entering Boalt do not necessarily approach law school as progressives. But those who do have made it possible for students of varying backgrounds and levels of political consciousness to educate themselves about the connections between the hierarchies of legal education and the historical exclusions of particular communities from institutions of power. At the same time, progressive law students face a different set of challenges than liberal and radical students.

Two stories illustrate both the successes and challenges of progressive student organizing beyond the law school study group that Kennedy advocates. At Boalt, the most dynamic and effective student group—and, not coincidentally, the student group most hated by the administration—has long been the Coalition for Diversity (the Coalition).[17] Where liberal and radical students must struggle against the sense of helplessness and hopelessness that Kennedy describes and move toward a sense of empowerment, progressive students in the Coalition often find their primary antagonist to be the liberal perspective, whether represented in other students, in the organizational structures of law school, or in themselves. While resisting the call of liberalism and radicalism, progressive students also struggle to build and maintain the solidarity and trust that coalition work requires.

Like many other student institutions, the Coalition waxes and wanes in strength and support from the student body. During the 2000–2001 academic year, students revitalized the Coalition after a period of relative inactivity[18] and began working on issues of faculty hiring, student admissions, and the curriculum. The incoming class of 2003 further revitalized the Coalition's anti-racist efforts, motivated by several factors. First, during this class's first semester, professors who were particularly dismissive of questions about race, gender, class, and other forms of difference were assigned to teach first-year courses. This resulted in much informal organizing for mutual support, such as women-of-color dinners and alternative reading groups. Second, this class contained a core group of strong, committed students of color who had background experience in organizing around issues of difference, as well as undergraduate educations informed by scholarship about the dynamics of difference and power and about ongoing struggles of racialized communities. Finally, the faculty's interest in hiring a scholar who had become notorious for his sensationalistic critiques of critical race and feminist theories became a flashpoint for organizing.[19]

The Coalition worked both to raise student consciousness about the implications of this professor's candidacy for efforts to improve race relations among faculty members and to provide a welcoming rather than hostile environment for students from minority racial groups. While the Coalition was not able to change the faculty's hiring decision, the incident provided the opportunity for students to think critically and to strategize about issues of "diversity." In their organizing work, Coalition students certainly drew on Kennedy's playbook, calling attention to the alienating effects of law school for a broad range of students, arguing that this hire would increase rather than decrease student alienation, and trying to encourage apathetic and timid students to make their voices heard. However, the Coalition students also looked beyond the law school, drawing on their commitment to communities that are underserved and underrepresented in the ranks of legal practitioners and academics.

The ultimate target in the Coalition campaign was neither the reform of legal education nor an attack on "hierarchy," broadly defined, but the campaign for racial justice. Thus, Coalition students sought to connect student feelings of disconnection and alienation at Boalt with the battle raging over racial issues beyond the law school, such as the fate of affirmative action in the federal courts. The Coalition's activities did not end with the failure of the campaign to keep a particular scholar from being hired. Instead, while the Coalition's in-your-face actions (such as a demonstration in the hallway outside the room where the faculty vote was taken, in which students wore tape over their mouths to symbolize their silencing) alienated some students, it radicalized others, creating new linkages among student groups concerning both racial issues and issues of student governance.

Indeed, much of the Coalition's groundwork paid off in the spring of 2003, when progressive students at Boalt, working with progressive students from other Bay Area law schools, organized a well-attended and successful conference bringing together social justice lawyers, activists, students, and scholars on the topic of coalition building itself. The conference brought into collaboration many student groups that had never worked together and furthered the Coalition's progressive ambitions: neither simply to implement liberal reforms at Boalt nor to bring about the revolution but to connect the student struggle with struggles beyond the law school's walls.

The solidarity-building successes of the Coalition, however, must be understood along with the challenges progressive students often face. In the spring of 2001, several progressive students (including Coalition members) decided to join the *California Law Review* (*CLR*). Their concern about *CLR* was classic Kennedy-plus-racial-justice progressive: the students were troubled about how the journal's demographic homogeneity narrowed Boalt's "pipeline" of credentialed students into academia, judicial clerkships, and other careers.[20] Their reasons for joining the journal were therefore not simply to individually obtain the benefits of membership (including institutional status and the perception of increased job opportunities) but also to increase access to these benefits to members of groups that are historically underrepresented on the journal. One of these students, a Latina, was elected as the first woman-of-color editor-in-chief in the journal's history. Four other progressive students won elected positions in other departments.

One of the priorities for transforming the journal was membership. The group wanted to raise issues about how membership selection methods might be contributing to the continued underrepresentation or absence of African American, Latino, and Native American students on the journal.[21] These discussions proved to be extremely difficult, however, because of the small number of members who were interested in examining the link between racial dynamics, assessments of "merit," and limitations in the membership as currently constituted. Despite the fact that there were no Black or Native American members and only two Latino/a members in the 2003 class of *CLR,* most journal members insisted that the journal was "race-neutral," that most members valued "diversity" (but not necessarily limited to racial diversity), and that attention to race would introduce "bias."

The progressive students also considered attempting to address the demographic homogeneity of the authors *CLR* publishes. Their concern, again, was about the pipeline: the career boost that publishing in prestigious law reviews provides. However, this homogeneity turned out to be even more difficult to change. Without sufficient numbers in the key departments to transform the journal's existing values—presumptions about the value of certain areas of law over others; assessments of "quality" that rely heavily on where the author went to school, where she or he teaches, and where he or she has published previously; and a lack of attention to areas of scholarly expertise that are more heavily populated by scholars of color and women—the journal continued to follow its majoritarian impulse toward the reproduction of exclusionary notions of excellence. Thus, for example, during the 2002–3 academic year while the progressive students served on *CLR,* of over twenty authors that the articles department selected, two were white women, one was a Black male, and one was an Asian American male.[22]

Not only conventionally liberal attitudes about race but also the institutional reproduction of hierarchy proved to be an obstacle in transforming *CLR.* A series of events surrounding the journal's diversity editor (DE) illustrates this problem. The membership of *CLR* had voted to establish a diversity editor position in 2001, subject to yearly renewal.[23] As DE, a member of the progressive group began proactively to develop a strategy to address the *Review*'s lack of diversity. In response to her work, this DE was the subject of much ridicule in *CLR*'s internal newsletter, resulting in a barrage of incidents of support and backlash regarding diversity.

While some members hoped to deal with the incidents in a way that would address the harm to diversity efforts on the journal, many Executive Committee and Editorial Board members relied on conservative readings of the organization's bylaws in ways that limited any constructive response to the events. Several journal members were able to use formal mechanisms of group decision making to resist any efforts to address "outsiders" (nonmembers) who had raised concerns about the incidents. What was never confronted was how the lack of diversity of membership contributed to an impoverished internal discussion about how to address the issues. In the end, three Editorial Board members resigned (all of whom had been members of the group attempting to transform the organization), and members of *CLR* voted not to renew the diversity editor position.

By attempting to work within the liberal, formally "neutral" structures of this elitist organization, the progressive students hit a wall of inertia that changed into severe backlash during their terms in office. Instead of finding ways to use the space they made at *CLR* to develop a critical consciousness that could confront the various forms of power operating to uphold multiple hierarchies, they fell into an abyss of organizational unchangeability. The obsession with formal structures and processes—designed, of course, for the reproduction of the institution according to the status quo—made it impossible to address the continuation of exclusions of persons belonging to historically underrepresented groups in any effective way. Progressive students could serve as an irritant by challenging the racial status quo, but this ultimately produced backlash against these particular individuals rather than institutional change.

One final observation about student organizing takes off from *CLR*'s successful self-reproduction. *Legal Education and the Reproduction of Hierarchy*, while touting the law school study group as the basic unit of student organized resistance, also describes in some detail the problems group action inevitably generates, including personality conflicts, the emergence of factions, and relations of domination within the group itself. Kennedy argues that neither giving up on group action nor institutionalizing the group to create a clear "chain of command" is a sufficient response, and he advocates instead for a form of open process such that responsibilities can rotate and disagreements can be tolerated without breaking up the group (129–33). The Coalition has certainly tried to maintain such an open process throughout its existence. One of the problems with this structure that Kennedy does not mention, however, is the problem of memory. Contrasting the Coalition with *CLR* makes this clear. There have been a number of efforts to sustain the memory of the Coalition's racial justice work over time, as generations of students pass through Boalt.[24] Yet the stories that are handed down are often limited to particular moments, such as the annual Coalition teach-in about the history of diversity at Boalt. It is always an uphill battle to preserve the Coalition's street knowledge and experience. In contrast, *CLR* maintains a recorded history in files, documents, correspondence, structural resolutions and voting results, and other records. One benefit, then, of some formal structure would be the development of institutional memory that would make it unnecessary for the Coalition to reinvent the wheel every three years.

In contrast *CLR*'s papers preserve only the history of hegemony: the core or center of the journal, not the resistances. Alternative memories are even more difficult to retrieve within *CLR* than within the Coalition since there have been no ongoing organizing efforts. There may be a sense, then, in which an authorized history is worse than none. Kennedy's intuition may be right that the costs of institutionalization ultimately outweigh the benefits.

Conclusion: Overlapping Hierarchies, Circulations of Power, and Constantly Critical Praxis

In the progressive view, power does not only reside in a top-down structure of hierarchy. Power also "produces things, . . . induces pleasure, forms knowledge, produces discourse. It needs to be considered as a productive network which runs through the whole social body."[25] Drawing from this conception of power, Foucault writes,

> [T]here are no relations of power without resistances; the latter are all the more real and effective because they are formed right at the point where re-lations of power are exercised; resistance to power does not have to come from elsewhere to be real, nor is it inexorably frustrated through being the compatriot of power. It exists all the more by being in the same place as power; hence, like power, resistance is multiple and can be integrated in global strategies.[26]

Measures of what counts as resistance and what counts as success are in-herently tied to the notion of power that is to be confronted. While the Coalition has not changed racial hierarchies at the school, it has created possibilities for its members to continue to develop constantly critical practices of resistance. Its loose structure and informality give the Coali-tion the flexibility to address effects of shifting circulations of power. The Coalition has developed the ability to mobilize and to strategize quickly when action is required, especially when necessary to support the work of other progressive and identity-based organizations at the school. While the Coalition's activist orientation has alienated some students, it has pos-itively affected the racial environment at Boalt. Even while it sometimes provides a lightning rod for anger, the Coalition also provides a measure of "safety" for other organizations and for students of color more gener-ally. Other students—and the administration—are well aware that the Coalition is capable of quick action when events happen that negatively affect people of color.

As the *CLR* example shows, the greatest obstacle to progressive action at Boalt is often not conservatism but liberalism. Yet the groundwork for progressive transformation has been laid even here. While efforts to chal-lenge hierarchy at the journal resulted in retrenchment, the hollowness of its assertions about "excellence" has become clearer for many students. The membership's very public backlash against "diversity" resulted in heightened attention from outside the organization, including from stu-dent-of-color groups. To maintain its elite status (since it has not been able to maintain a code of secrecy about its reactions to attempts to end historical exclusions of persons from underrepresented minority groups),[27] *CLR* now must attend to the fact that "outsiders," such as vocal and visible Coalition members, have a different interpretation from the enclosed, internal meanings that require secrecy, erasure, and the continued absence of persons with knowledge of the operations of racialized hierarchies. While the journal may be able to continue along its current path, the irritations of counterdiscourse make more visible the disjunctures between elitist claims to excellence and actions that reproduce ignorance and exclusion.

Efforts by progressive students to transform hierarchies indicate the importance of constant resistance, and also the usefulness of a midlevel political analysis: not focusing on the law school (the local) as a fulcrum for changing the world (the global) but understanding legal education as one aspect of very particular social struggles for justice. The Coalition for Diversity in some ways is the embodiment of the kind of resistance Kennedy advocates. Its diffuse structure and efforts have enabled members to figure out how to connect issues, to constantly look for complex relationships of the operations of power, and to set in motion dynamics of change even beyond specific, planned actions. The organization's success may at times appear small, but the complexity of power relationships indicates the necessity of such small, constant resistances. Such organizing work, which contributes to the development of complex critical perspectives and coalition-building skills, as well as lessons learned by efforts to change the most elite, hierarchical structures (such as law review), may help prepare such students for struggles in the hierarchically ordered liberal legal-political world we inhabit.

At the same time, progressive students in the Coalition and elsewhere add to Kennedy's two left stances an ability to treat law as only one thread in a web of relations of power and to bring their prior experiences of subordination, resistance, and critical thinking directly to bear on their law school organizing. Both the liberal and radical stances Kennedy describes understand the law as the law understands itself: as, for good or ill, the foundation of the house of power. This view, however, sustains power relations by appealing only to the realm of law itself for resistance. The belief that law school, the legal profession, and the law more generally are the sole, or even key, places for reproducing or undoing hierarchy sets up this realm as the most significant place for work in confronting power, so that people with legal skills continue to be held up as the most important actors for social change.

As an alternative, progressive law students may use their involvement with the law to participate in broader resistance practices. We have focused on connecting resistance against legal hierarchy with the fight for racial justice, but of course there are many other kinds of anti-subordination struggles that can serve as the basis for a valuable praxis. Kennedy's assessment of the circuits of institutional self-replication remains a valuable one; but left students who come to law school need not choose between liberal naïveté and radical alienation. Instead, law students may draw on their experiences of hierarchy outside legal education to transform their conditions of life, grounded in the knowledge of the necessity of constant struggle and resistance.

NOTES

1. *See* LAURA STEVENS, LAW SCHOOL: LEGAL EDUCATION IN AMERICA FROM THE 1850S TO THE 1980S 39 (1983).

2. As Deborah Rhode puts it succinctly, at the beginning of the twenty-first century, "Attorneys serving low-income clients and public interest causes cope with staggering caseloads and grossly inadequate resources." DEBORAH L. RHODE, IN THE INTERESTS OF JUSTICE: REFORMING THE LEGAL PROFESSION 29 (2000).

3. For an effort to make the Third World Strike visible in the history of critical race theory, *see* Sumi Cho and Robert Westley, *Critical Race Coalitions: Key Movements That Performed the Theory,* 33 U.C. DAVIS L. REV. 1377 (2000) (hereafter *Critical Race Coalitions*).

4. *See* generally GARY B. NASH, CHARLOTTE CRABTREE, AND ROSS E. DUNN, HISTORY ON TRIAL: CULTURE WARS AND THE TEACHING OF THE PAST (1997).

5. *Id.* at 234.

6. *Id.* at 99.

7. *See* SHERENE RAZACK, LOOKING WHITE PEOPLE IN THE EYE (1998).

8. As Edward Said puts it, "[W]e can better understand the persistence and the durability of saturating hegemonic systems like culture when we realize that their internal constraints upon writers and thinkers were *productive,* not unilaterally inhibiting." EDWARD SAID, ORIENTALISM 139 (1994).

9. The exception that proves the rule is a fascinating passage in which Kennedy devotes two paragraphs to female, working-class, and black students' experience, suggesting that for them, law school is more of the same (82). This is followed by a funny and fascinating account of the sexual politics, circa 1983, of the "annual dinner of a student honor society," which Kennedy compares to the senior prom (83–84). This latter passage is the only point where the "you" being addressed in the essay really clearly has a gender (male) and a race (white); and the stiffness of the race/class/gender discussion, compared with the easy fluidity and familiarity

with which Kennedy addresses "you," supports the inference that Kennedy's imaginary reader is a straight white male student for whom being alienated and subordinated is a new experience.

10. *See* Angela P. Harris, *The Jurisprudence of Reconstruction,* 82 CALIF. L. REV. 741 (1994). Patricia Williams, one of the pioneers of critical race theory, said it beautifully:

> To say that blacks never fully believed in rights is true. Yet it is also true that blacks believed in them so much and so hard that we gave them life where there was none before; we held onto them, put the hope of them into our wombs, mothered them and not the notion of them. And this was not the dry process of reification, from which life is drained and reality fades as the cement of conceptual determinism hardens round—but its opposite. This was the resurrection of life from ashes four hundred years old. The making of something out of nothing took immense alchemical fire—the fusion of a whole nation and the kindling of several generations.

PATRICIA J. WILLIAMS, THE ALCHEMY OF RACE AND RIGHTS: DIARY OF A LAW PROFESSOR 163 (1991).

11. Luke W. Cole, *Macho Law Brains, Public Citizens, and Grassroots Activists: Three Models of Environmental Advocacy,* 14 VA. ENVTL L.J. 687, 703 (1995) (hereafter *Macho Law Brains*).

12. The environmental justice movement found its voice at the People of Color Leadership Summit in Washington, D.C., in 1991, and that the movement is both critical of law and lawyers and led largely by people of color and white women is no accident. Activists concerned about toxic hazards to poor and minority communities found it difficult to gain a hearing with the mainstream environmental movement, which had concerned itself primarily with wilderness preservation and endangered species. *See generally* CONFRONTING ENVIRONMENTAL RACISM: VOICES FROM THE GRASSROOTS (Robert D. Bullard ed., 1993)

13. *Macho Law Brains, supra* note 11, at 701–2.

14. *Id.* at 697.

15. *Id.* at 707.

16. GERALD P. LOPEZ, REBELLIOUS LAWYERING: ONE CHICANO'S VISION OF PROGRESSIVE LAW PRACTICE (1992).

17. For one account of the Coalition's founding, see *Critical Race Coalitions, supra* note 3.

18. A period of unusual student and faculty inactivity, even apathy, concerning issues of racial justice occurred at Boalt after the passage of SP-1 and SP-2 and Proposition 209. As Kaaryn Gustafson, an African American student at Boalt at the time, writes:

> Beyond the fact that Berkeley was failing to fulfill its promise that my generation of minority students would be followed by yet another, was the fact that most of the faculty and administrators, and even many of the students on campus,

simply remained idle—disengaged from the moral battle to define the common good, wilfully ignorant of the practical social effects of affirmative action's end, and contributing to a vast field of paralyzing indifference.
Kaaryn Gustafson, *Broken Promises*, 13 BERKELEY WOMEN'S L.J. 3, 5 (1998).

19. *See, e.g.,* Daniel Farber and Suzanna Sherry, *Is the Radical Critique of Merit Anti-Semitic?* 83 CALIF. L. REV. 853 (1995). In this article, Farber and Sherry deploy Jewish and Asian American identities to argue that critical race and feminist perspectives on merit reproduce the anti-Semitism that led to the Holocaust. Dr. Sherry was not involved in the Boalt controversy.

20. Donna writes as a member of the Coalition during this time and as one of the students who attempted to transform *CLR*.

21. The current membership selection process includes a casenote, a personal statement, and a bluebooking exercise.

22. One of the pieces authored by a woman author was part of a collection accepted as a group and the other was a piece coauthored with two men. In other words, during the 2002–3 academic year, the department did not select a single article by an individual woman author.

23. The mandate for the DE was "to collect statistical data regarding membership composition, to research the effects of Proposition 209 on *CLR*'s membership selection process, to communicate with other student groups and the Boalt administration on diversity issues, to encourage *CLR* members to discuss issues of diversity, to organize additional committees or groups to discuss such issues, and to propose changes and/or structural resolutions if appropriate"; in other words, to "analyze those factors that enhance or inhibit diversity within *CLR*." Amy De-Vaudreuil, *Silence at the California Law Review,* 91 CALIF. L. REV. (2003), quoting the Diversity Editor Structural Resolution (Feb. 5, 2001).

24. Cho and Westley's essay about the Coalition provides an important recorded history of the organization; *see Critical Race Coalitions, supra* note 3. This essay is supplemented by Andrea Guerrero's book SILENCE AT BOALT HALL: THE DISMANTLING OF AFFIRMATIVE ACTION (2002) and by the work of individuals such as Kaaryn Gustafson (author of *Broken Promises, supra* note 18), who remains at Boalt while completing a Ph.D. and continues to provide a great deal of institutional memory for students about the history of the Coalition and its work.

25. MICHEL FOUCAULT, POWER/KNOWLEDGE: SELECTED INTERVIEWS & OTHER WRITINGS 1972–1977 119 (Colin Gordon ed., 1980).

26. *Id.* at 142.

27. It is important to note that this representation of "what happened" is not accepted by most members of *CLR*. Discourse about the events center on assertions that no one is against diversity; most members resist the casting of the events as efforts to "desegregate" or end historic exclusions.

Of Time and the Pedagogy
of Critical Legal Studies

Janet Halley

Legal Education and the Reproduction of Hierarchy (*LERH*) is now[1] two decades old. When Duncan published it in 1983, I was an English professor. At the time I was quite unmindful of how the ideas and practices then collected under the rubric "Critical Legal Studies"—ideas and practices of many people, not just Duncan, as he indicates repeatedly in that text—crystallized and instigated a certain kind of turmoil in the legal academy. Perhaps at the very moment (certainly in the same year) that *LERH* first appeared in its nifty red cover, I was holed in at the British Library reading radical Protestant pamphlets from the English Civil War—Shakers, Diggers, mortalists, regicides, antinomians—the whole rabble of Christopher Hill's "Protestant Revolution." I recall that now because there is much in my encounter this year (it is my first encounter) with *LERH* that repeats my experience in the Thomason Tracts, at the Huntington Library, in various serene libraries holding the paper traces of a huge social upheaval.

Let us suppose me in 1983 reading Gerrard Winstanley's *The Law of Freedom*[2] and me in 2003 reading *LERH*. Does this juxtaposition help me see what it means for *LERH* to reemerge in this elegant, necessarily retrospective yet very "now" New York University Press imprint?

Well, both Janet Halleys would say that both texts, with their low production values and their coterie-press intimacy, provoke a vivid sense of their own social and temporal immediacy (that once was). The Little Red Book deviates in almost every possible way from the Joe Christiansen, Inc., product. In its 1983 avatar it is literally little and red; its page format is almost square (seven inches—it's a tract, a pamphlet, a chapbook); the binding is two large staples that press deep into the paper; the typeface mimics the typeface of a typewriter (a deliberate anachronism, as the text is right-justified and therefore must have been produced on a word processor); the inset images are clearly "cutouts" from elsewhere, made and found objects, and highly allusive rather than directly illustrative. The letters of the title march across the front cover in rigid banners, without kerning[3]—calling attention to themselves *as letters,* obscuring their merger into *words,* arraying themselves in rows like the stripes on a flag, and generally screaming for attention.

All of these aesthetic details except the use of a color cover (not just any color; it's *red,* a direct reference to Mao's Little Red Book) belong as well to the radical tracts of the Puritan Revolution. The visitor to the Beinecke Library, the Rare Book Room at the Huntington Library, or some other posh retreat is offered crumbling, hastily sewn together quires of paper—paper that is itself so inelegantly made as to seem sometimes corrugated; little blobs of unpulverized wood or flax sometimes pry themselves loose, and you look up terrified lest the librarian blame you! The handset type is unkerned, some letters appearing upside down or gone missing altogether; lines appear in the wrong places and paragraphs are sometimes repeated; the pagination and even the order of pages are rife with error; woodcut images of the most striking and the most puzzling intensity recall the elegant illuminations in bygone scribal manuscripts, but do so in the catachrestic visual imagery of the then-popular "emblem" books of sententious literature and in the technical patois of proto–mass production. The title page is a screed of bold announcements, all stacked one on top of the other in serried ranks differentiated by every variation in font size and type at the typesetter's disposal, and squeezed in so tight and with so little regard for legibility that the modern reader sees in them a forerunner not of the book cover but of the "screamer" headlines of the tabloid press the day after *huge* news has broken.

So each of these texts deviates from its contemporary aesthetic conventions for highbrow publication in ways that invite me to see them as ephemeral, as interventions in and of a moment. To hold them is to catch the past like a fly in amber, to whiff an aroma sealed until now in an amphora. And so you immediately notice that the fly is not moving; you wonder if the wine has gone way off (and who would verify that for you?). That is, the paradox of sheer immediacy and sheer pastness is graphically heightened when one confronts sophisticated ephemera of the sort we have here; it is heightened to a near crisis when those emphemera are *newly reprinted* for fresh circulation, as *LERH* is in the present volume.

I'll never forget reading Christopher Hill's *Milton and the English Revolution*.[4] This would have been while I was in graduate school at UCLA—Duncan would then have been beginning his work on classical legal thought, on left law-and-economics analysis; he was also working out the analysis of the law school classroom and corporate firm that are incorporated in the Little Red Book. I was writing about the poet and pampleteer John Milton. Trained by old historicists who thought that reading canonical texts from the past meant finding out "the historical meaning" and "the intention" of the text, and by new critics who decried all that as the "intentional fallacy" and urged "close reading" of the "text itself," I was groping for some way to read historically and politically without giving up on the textual quality of texts. Hill's book broke in on me like a waterfall. He was not a particularly subtle reader of literature, but what an astounding mind he had for accreting the archival traces of the social, intellectual, and political activities of a deeply politically engaged, socially alive, self-revising writer like Milton! He marshaled trace after trace of Milton's social/political/intellectual/religious life, all taken together showing that Milton had once *lived*—lived in a tumultuous world in which he helped make the tumult. I know this sounds incredible, but this was a completely new idea to me. Diaries, letters, broadsides, pamphlets gave evidence of the radical Protestants Milton knew, the coffeehouses where they convened day after day to talk—about what? one would love to know; one could only imagine their minute attentiveness to one another's most recent pamphlet or sermon. No more could Hill catch the fly of their talk than he could of their feelings and their thought—instead, it was as though he held the amber up against a strong light and, by the resulting shadow on the wall, suggested how silent, now, are those once-urgent voices.

It is precisely the analogue of this everyday practice of intellectual sociability—the mid-seventeenth-century London radical Protestant version of which Hill could only allude to, never revive, by immensely detailed work in the archive—that I will never know about Critical Legal Studies (CLS) in its sociable golden age. You can see the traces all over *Legal Education and the Reproduction of Hierarchy;* but at every one, the smell of the library comes over me, and I wonder: What *don't* I know about this? For instance, Duncan repeatedly thanks the group for generating the ideas set

forth here but always attaches a careful proviso assuming solitary responsibility. I can just imagine the communal floggings that must have happened if these acknowledgments and disavowals were not performed *just
right;* or is that my own fear of merger, my shyness, my envy, projecting itself on a past now irretrievably gone? Chapter 9 provides an edgy "insider's" description of the techniques of leadership—when to indulge,
when to ostracize solo flyers; when to seem to follow, when to leap into action; and so forth. And I wonder: Didn't Duncan worry that people would
remember these tips at the next meeting and see him not as an organic
participant but as a cool manipulator, and resist *him?* Was his radicalism
expressed precisely in offering this capacity to anyone who would simply
read to the end? *Is there* such a thing as nonhierarchical leadership? The
tract closes with a set of recipes for student activism—but could it really
be rebellious if the students needed a recipe to figure it out? Wouldn't then
they need to rebel *against the recipe?* If they never did what Duncan suggested they do, was that rebellion or indifference? If they did what he suggested, how rebellious could it be, really? After all, law school clinics of the
sort envisioned here have not changed the world much, and have done
much to foster just the attitudes of charity and despair that Duncan decries in *LERH.*

If the past present of *LERH* is opaque to me now, the text's presence in
the present brings that opacity forward. The Little Red Book closes with a
short bibliography of superclassic readings, complete with an offer to contact Duncan at his Harvard address for a "much longer, free Bibliography"
and the coda inviting readers' interest in the Conference on Critical Legal
Studies and offering Mark Tushnet at what appears to be his (then) *actual
home address* for information about meetings, conferences, summer retreats, the mailing list. Both of these suggest rich nodes of sociability
woven by texts of various kinds; both hold forth the promise of intense
face-to-face social forms. Since 1983, much of the textual stroking has
moved to the Web—a cooler but cheaper medium—and I will say that I
find that many survivors of CLS's golden age are remarkable for their appetite for—and ability to foster in others the appetite for, the flexibility to
generate, the stamina to withstand—new forms of face-to-face social/political/intellectual life for left legal intellectuals. But the degree to which
that capacity "continues" something in CLS is not, for me, a fact we can
"know"; any claims one way or the other—"CLS is dead"; "CLS lives"—
would be, to borrow Eric Hobsbawm's priceless phrase, an "invention of
tradition."[5]

So let's consign *LERH* decisively to the past; and let's assume for ourselves the explicitly new historicist posture of *managers* of the past we've just sent it to. What more, then, can we say about its formal repetition of a style of radical publication from centuries past? One idea would be to return to Hill, who, in describing the superheated social milieu of mid-seventeenth-century London, also describes a world in which printing certain unorthodox ideas was prohibited. Like Catholics under Elizabeth and James, the radical Protestants resorted to pseudonymous publication on surreptitious presses that could be dismantled and reassembled quickly—literally "fly by night." It was an era of the "no imprint imprint." Anyone reading in the Thomason Tracts repeatedly wonders, "Who wrote this? Who printed it? How many editions? How was it distributed? Anything missing from this copy? How did this get into a library? *What is the sociability of this text?*" The same questions, adjusted a bit to be sure, would be asked about *samizdat,* early translations of the Bible into everyday languages, indeed (take away the printing press), the early manuscripts of the Christian gospels.

Coming to *LERH* with *these* priors, I was intrigued by its mysterious imprint. Of course, it is not anonymous. "Duncan Kennedy" is no pseudonym—we may not *know* who he is or was, but his authorial persona clearly appears as the performer of this writing; to read it as a work by Duncan Kennedy is to weave it into anything else we think we know about that person. But the title page draws directly (even if "unintentionally") on the tradition of radical Protestant tracts (and other "illegitimate" modes of textual production) when it asks us to believe that the Little Red Book issues from the publishing house "AFAR."[6]

From AFAR? You could convince me that there was a publisher with the tradename Afar in 1983, but you'd have to work pretty hard to do it. Instead, I think, we are to understand that this little red book comes "from afar."[7] And where might "afar" be? The images I have already referred to suggest two answers.

The first, more accessible one emphasizes the sheer mystery of this name. Blazoned on the back of the front (and again on the front of the back) cover we find a bright (bright red, that is) ringed planet floating alone in a waste of black ink—oops, I mean, black space. The text originates not "no where" ("utopia" in Greek is *u-topos,* "no place") but somewhere, albeit somewhere far, far away.[8]

And then there are the two images carefully (full copyright regalia here) attributed to Beatrix Potter's children's story *The Tale of Two Bad*

Mice.[9] As I've suggested, these hark back, for me, to the highly allusive emblem woodcuts that adorned so many publications in the mid–seventeenth century, and that appeared as well in the radical Protestant pamphlets. Like the emblems introducing so many of the old books I have handled, moreover, they seem to reward deep iconographic acquaintance with the image and its textual trajectory, and to depend on a highly abstruse verbal/visual pun.[10]

As we all know, children's stories often begin "A long time ago and far far away"—but *The Tale of Two Bad Mice* doesn't. Instead it begins, "Once upon a time there was a very beautiful doll's house . . . "; and we see an image of a doll's house that must have seemed, to middle-class British readers in 1904, utterly quotidian, mundane, everyday to the last degree. The story brings the "afar" into daily life, however: it works magic into the problem of appearance and reality in everyday life. The work begins on the first page, where we read that this doll's house "was red brick with white windows, and it had *real* muslin curtains."[11] OK. So the doll's house is *not* real, but it *contains* real muslin curtains? What's going on?

The basic structure of the answer appears in the two dolls who inhabit the house. One is a clearly artificial stick doll with a fixed, startled expression; the other is a highly naturalistic doll always posed in a luxuriously emotional stance that, though identical every time she appears, also seems always intensely responsive and *à propos*. When I first saw them, I took the former to be "the doll" and the latter to be "the girl"; only reluctantly did I relinquish the lavishly expressive figure to the domain of the unreal.[12] This transition through the aperture between the real and the unreal is the basic narrative vocabulary of the story.

It all starts when the dolls go on an outing. Promptly the two bad mice—none other than Tom Thumb and his wife, Hunca Munca—sneak in and sit down at the table (which is, of course, *just the right size*) to feast on the resplendent meal the dolls have left behind. The mice are quickly enraged to find that the ham, the fish, all of it was made of "nothing but plaster." That is, for them, the luscious meal shifts—just as the femmy, animated doll did for me—from the real to the fake. And they are enraged. They go on the rampage, breaking up the enameled simulacra of food, pouring the glass beads out of the "Rice" and "Coffee" canisters, tossing clothes out of drawers. It is the world turned upside down, a revolt against the fake on behalf of a longed-for real. But the fake has its own stern realities. When the mice cram the fish into the "red hot crinkly paper fire" in the grate—"it would not burn." Tom Thumb, so taken aback by this that he climbs up inside the chimney to see what is going wrong, appears at the top with a dazed expression: "there was no soot"! And finally, in the person of Hunca Munca, they realize that the unreal might also be real (remember, the dollhouse has "*real* muslin curtains"): pulling the feathers out of a bolster to strew them ruinously throughout the house, her "frugal mind" suddenly re-sees the fake as real: "she remembered that she herself was in want of a feather bed."

This transition sets the stage for the next moment in the political education of the mice: the looting. Across the rug and into the mouse house go the bolster, a chair, a cradle, pots, pans, a dress—but not, of course, the things too big to fit through their much smaller door. Of course not those.

Let's check in once again with "the reader." The doll's house with its everyday magic holds the privileged place, initially, of the child's tale's "far, far away." We accept, because we love moving into the magic of the bedtime story, the implausible humanness of these mice, the folly of supposing that two dolls own the dollhouse, and so on. But when the mice rise up in rage against the artificiality of the very things we lovingly accepted as the stuff of delightful fiction, they become protagonists; it becomes possible not merely to behold them but *to identify with them* as they launch themselves up a learning curve. Once they do, we rejoice in their violent debunking of the dolls' house; we share their bafflement when the very objects just moments ago revealed to be fake become intransigently real (and will not burn); and we feel the rush of power and capacity that comes when they finally master the real/fake distinction and loot the house for real things they can really use. The mice are no longer hilarious idiots; they have become savvy actors—and we identify with them most triumphally precisely at the moment that their destructive rampage becomes purposive, appropriative, *political.*

This is the moment (as the Protestant radicals studied by Christopher Hill imagined it) of "the world turn'd up side down."[13] It is a crucial trope of comedy—the Lord of Misrule, Dionysius, bacchanal—and a crucial trope in the imagery of revolution.[14] The real and the unreal merge in the climax of the mouse rebellion, when they bring the doll's house, or parts of it, back home with them; they pull the "real" away from the adult, human world and through the aperture of a mouse's eye; it has gone "afar." That is now our world too, and until the last two pages of the story we see reality from inside it. And it is a place of complete social triumph.

Triumph that is not to last. The second crisis in the story arrives when the dolls return and confront the destruction in mute awe. And more ominously still, the humans make their first appearance:

> The little girl that the doll's house belonged to said: "I will get a doll dressed like a policeman!" And the nurse said, "I will set a mouse-trap!"

These are the story bits that belong to Duncan's two images. Not only are the dolls back; the humans to whom they are mere dolls are suddenly active in the story. The scope across which the mice must master the fake/real distinction has been vastly expanded: flat doll/round doll; dollhouse/real muslin curtains; fish/fire; fire/bolster; mice/dolls; and, finally, all of the above/real live human beings wielding statelike power.

The illustrations accompanying these story moments in the text are apt illustrations for *LERH* exactly because they do *not* depict the real, human girl getting a policeman doll or the real, human nurse setting a real mousetrap. By the time our images are "taken," those acts have already occurred, and we see the sequel in the political life of the two bad mice. It's not the real (the state) against the fake (the mice); rather, the problem of the real and the unreal is now a problem inside the mice. Indeed, in these images Tom Thumb and Hunca Munca appear as masters and teachers, fully apprised of the complex world they now live in. Hunca Munca stands before the overbearingly tall policeman doll, holding her baby up to look him in the eye: it is a defiant, fearless stance. And Tom Thumb, backed up by Hunca Munca anxiously hovering with babe in arms, addresses three childish mice while gesticulating at a hulking mousetrap; the kid mice are paying rapt attention. She must be teaching her infant something, but what? To face up to, or to see though the illusion of, state power? He must be teaching the mouselets how to remain undeceived, but how? To fear the terrible mechanical engine of the moustrap, or to decompose it into parts and treat it like a silly threat, a plaything like the doll's house? Parent and child, teacher and student, are bonded together in a knowledge project which, if successful, will render the mousetrap a mere box of wood—but which, if it fails, will involve them all in its power to break their little necks.

For all that Duncan identifies more with Hunca Munca in his Afterword to this book,[15] he has put the image of Tom Thumb teaching the kids about the mousetrap on the cover of another self-published volume[16] which contains, before this, the only readily accessible reproduction of *LERH*. I will come back to this double image in his self-representation in a moment.

The textual status of the subsequent volume will, I think, help us. It is a collection of Xeroxes of Duncan's own work on legal education, starting with *LERH* and including, in otherwise chronological order, ten papers that he published in law reviews between 1970 and 1995. Certain scandalous essays which were never published, but which I have seen from time to time as photocopies of typescript, are not included; nor is *Lizard*, the *newspaper*—yes, *newspaper*—that Duncan (and others?) published as the daily record of the 1984 Association of American Law Schools Conference, and in particular of the CLS incursion into it.[17] No, the volume I have in hand includes (aside from *LERH*) the more "legitimate" works of Professor Kennedy on the subject of legal education. The cover follows the conventions of book publication: it is red; it is headed by the title *Essays on Legal Education;* Duncan's name then appears just where you would expect the name of the author; then (reading down the page) comes the image of Tom Thumb and the mousetrap from *Two Bad Mice* (with attribution; this is the "cover art" we have come to expect on book jackets); and then, at the bottom of the sheet, the date: January 1, 1996. There is no imprint. The cover and the text inside are obviously photocopied; the page format is what we now call "portrait," single sheet to a page, on eight-by-eleven standard copying paper; and it is perfect bound. He has made other anthologies in the same format, collecting his work under titles like *Left Wing Law and Economics* and *Essays on Adjudication, 1973–1996.* Allowing for the deviations necessary to produce them cheaply and distribute them for free, these are much more conventional, booklike products than the Little Red Book (or the explicit *samizdat*, or *Lizard*). Stacks of these various self-published collections are available for free, to any curious person, on the file cabinet outside his office. I am sure that if you request it he would send you a copy of any or all of them; if you have access to funds, you should offer to pay postage, as there is no outside funding.

The term *vanity press* captures something about this self-publication project, but not much. Strictly, I gather, a vanity press is a real commercial publishing house that produces small print runs of people's manuscripts, without editorial services (or interference) and for a fee. The output resembles much more closely the books produced by the big academic and trade presses than anything Duncan has done with a Xerox machine. The "vanity" moniker must arise at some nexus between the lack of market demand for a particular text and the author's (or promoter's) willingness to pay to secure some of the trappings of legitimacy that market demand would have secured for it. The Little Red Book in its avatar as itself, and as the introductory segment of *Essays on Legal Education,* conspicuously lacks these trappings; there is no pretense that anyone other than Duncan thought you should read it, far less that anyone decided that publishing it would be at least a break-even project financially. Still, there is something undeniably *vain*—especially in the senses that it is at once self-admiring and futile[18]—about the modes of self-publication Duncan has invented for himself. Especially when they reach booklike form, they implicitly insist both on the marginality of the work and on its crucial importance. It has no legitimacy and is something we really ought to take seriously into account. All told, there is both an abjection and a grandiosity in Duncan's adoption of these modes of book production and distribution.

Indeed, this paradoxicality may be what most strongly links the textual form of the Little Red Book to pamphlet production in prerevolutionary England. J. W. Saunders's famous 1951 article in *Essays in Criticism* argued that, at least in late-sixteenth-century England, a (male) courtier or would-be courtier (that is, participant in the center of power, the Court of the Prince) more or less had to write poetry, and had to circulate it among a carefully controlled coterie in order to produce its peculiar and proper range of meanings, and especially its distinctive sociability; but he had to circulate it in manuscript, as any apparent effort to obtain fame, and definitely any effort to *print* it, would be seen as the act of a parvenu and would brand him with the "stigma of print."[19] Of course manuscript production and circulation were, in the early years of the age of print, increasingly impractical and démodé and were directly inconsistent with the actual aims of many courtiers, as "courtier" was increasingly a career for self-made men who needed money and recognition and who at that time could get both by writing poetry; and indeed, most of the poetry we still have from the period was at one point or another printed. Against this backdrop the profusion of pamphlets in the prerevolutionary period was specifically bourgeois and explicitly and profusely wallowed in the stigma of print. Each pamphlet, however ephemeral, however notorious, however secretly or publicly distributed, bore the "meaning" of its author's confidence that it was of crucial public importance among a class then lurching toward a discovery of its mode of political power—and of his (sometimes her) needy and shameless pursuit of that public's attention.

All the more revealing, then, that Duncan deployed as his "emblematic devices" the two pedagogic images I have discussed from the near-conclusion of *Two Bad Mice,* but not the closing scenes themselves. Here are the last two segments of the story, with my descriptions of the accompanying images that appear before each facing page of text:

[The dolls are in bed—asleep?—and Hunca Munca and Tom Thumb stand together at the foot of the bed peering into a stocking, while Tom puts a coin in it.] So that is the story of the two Bad Mice. But they were not so very very naughty after all, because Tom Thumb paid for everything he broke. He found a crooked sixpense [*sic*] under the hearth-rug; and upon Christmas Eve he and Hunca Munca stuffed it into one of the stockings of Lucinda and Jane.

[Hunca Munca, bearing broom and dustpan, opens the door of the doll's house and steps over the threshold.] And very early every morning—before anybody is awake—Hunca Munca comes with her dust-pan and her broom to sweep the Dollies' house! THE END

The mice abandon strategies of outright rebellion (despoiling the doll's house), appropriation (stealing the dolls' things for their own house), and critique (seeing through and thus possibly disarming the police doll and the mousetrap) and turn instead to a strategy of compliance, infiltration, and undetectable subversion. They pay the dolls for the destruction they have wrought (compliance) with the dolls' own debased coin (undetectable subversion); and they retain the dolls' trust even to the extent that Hunca Munca can enter their house before anyone is awake (infiltration, threat), but only on terms that she sweep up the dolls' modest leavings (economic subordination, domestic servitude mode). Moreover, in the last scene we see Hunca Munca from a perspective inside the house: her head and the broom are silhouetted against the bright morning air; the dolls are not visible; and so the invitation is there, I think, to see her from the perspective of the unwary dolls. My own almost reflex reaction is to supply on their behalf the anxious mistrust mixed with cringing dependency that marked the attitude of the nineteenth-century British *haute bourgeoisie* toward its domestic servants. Perhaps this shift in identification is a fatal indication of my mother's fervent wish that I had been born with a silver spoon in my mouth, and of her mother's nostalgia for the days when she had servants. Ahem. I am told by more steadfast identifiers with the working class that the scene can be read with great anxiety for Hunca Munca as she enters to labor for her daily bread on what is basically enemy territory. This ambiguity aside, at the very least the last page of the book returns us to "reality" by implicitly admonishing its readers—good bourgeois children—that the mice are acceptable heroes because they were not, in the end, "very very naughty." We depart from the text reassured that rebellion is the stuff of play, nighttime fantasy, and the unreal, and that in the plain light of day we either fear and resent the servants for the trust we are forced to (mis)place in them or simply end up doing the sweeping.

These are very indicative outtakes. Writing from "afar" Duncan celebrates the two bad mice in their modes of rebellion, appropriation, and critique and embraces them in their magic transversal of the line between the real and the fake. The coincidence seems to be the point: given the relentless impingements of the police, the mousetrap, the little human girl, and the nurse, the possibility of rebellion, appropriation, and critique does seem to require a weird confluence of reality with the fantastic. It relies on the paradoxical. And Duncan just utterly neglects the mice—he silently amputates them from his project—when they make their peace with bourgeois morality while embracing a politics of invidious but meek infiltration.

Of course, that is what most of the students so vividly imagined in Duncan's Introduction to this book will actually do. They will not keep vigil with Duncan, waiting for the light of a new rebellion to break in the east. They will go to work for liberalism, intending to reform it from within, and end up meekly paying in their boss's coin for their transgressions and congratulating themselves for earning the trust owed to a good and faithful servant. The inducements to this approach are considerable, for power in the law school world has been consolidated in the center and is substantially shared among administrators, centrist faculty, and students who make the bargain from which Duncan, when he omitted the last two panels of the saga of the bad mice, averted his eyes.

Consider how effectively this coalition has captured the agenda produced by the student uprising in legal pedagogy that Duncan and many others of his generation fomented. The crits' "no-hassle pass" and their withering critique of socratic bullying have been reanimated as a new centrist norm that good teaching makes students comfortable and presents a full array of "points of view," as if they were commodities among which one might shop. The left feminist attack on sexual exploitation of students by teachers has produced the concept of a "hostile environment," which has gradually become the mantra of students whose radicalism consists in passive-aggressive attacks on the educational milieus they construct as commodities they have paid for and are entitled to consume without risking "trauma." If teachers include more race- and gender-oriented materials, we do so under the mandate that the materials provide optional "points of view" and that we remain responsible for ensuring that they do no one any harm. The crit intuition that students are agents, and politically responsible agents, in legal education has been supplanted in all these formulations by the centrist intuition that they are the recipients and consumers of it. Meanwhile, mandatory pro bono policies shift clinical work from the radical fringe of legal education toward its sentimental, charitable core; virtue is now required of everyone. And affirmative action is now justified on the constitutional level and managed institutionally not as an attack on an economically skewed, viciously distorting merit system but as the best means for elite institutions to find and allocate among themselves the students of color who can be most smoothly incorporated into the centrist coalition.[20] And so on.

If that is an important part of the context of the present republication of *LERH,* and for me it is, it is fascinating to note in Duncan's Introduction and Afterword a repetition of his gesture of omitting the last two frames of *The Tale of Two Bad Mice,* in a quite sustained gesture of "looking away" from his own students' agency in promoting and institutionalizing their lack of agency in legal education. Maybe criticizing students is just a bad idea and I'll come to regret it. It has a little bit of phallic sternness to it. And could Tom Thumb be threatening to spank the kid mice if they mess with the mousetrap? Surely this image of paternal pedagogy— Tom Thumb impending over his older kids, charging them with some very arresting knowledge, and protecting Hunca Munca and her infant from the heavy business of adult danger, as Hunca Munca stands behind her man and protects her infant from his gaze—corresponds well with the teacherly persona assumed by the author of *Essays on Legal Education;* a key entry in that volume, after all, is "Psycho-Social CLS," with its elaboration not only of the oedipal struggle waged between paternal mentors and their parricidal academic sons but also of the highly oblique entry point by which women academics gain access to the struggle.[21]

In his Afterword to this volume, Duncan shifts his affiliation to Hunca Munca. Not surprising. Here we have *LERH,* finally published by a legitimate, indeed a burgeoning academic press, under the editorial supervision

of two scholars who have undeniable stature on the left of the legal intelligentsia. We have commentaries in the style of a *Festschrift*. We have sewn
signatures, case bound; we have hardback copies on acid-free paper; we
have a copy in the Library of Congress. My e-mail inbox records Duncan's
struggle—over everything from page dimensions to typeface to black-
and-white (not color!) reproduction of the Potter prints—to secure the
distribution of *LERH* in this format without voicing the superflux of legitimacy that it bestows. But now his Little Red Book is encased in all the regalia of contemporary book dignity. Meanwhile, deep inside there, the text
still argues away, seeking to pry us loose from the very presuppositions
that make its newfound formal legitimacy possible: the idea of objective
and personal merit, and the idea that merit is transparently reproduced in
a vertical array of socially dominant and socially subordinate elements.
Self-publication of the sort Duncan devised for the Little Red Book *per-
forms* the critique of academic merit, and it gains authority only if it re-
cruits readers to its cell in the fluid cell structure of hierarchy. Grandiosity
and abjection merge there, in a form of power that both exerts itself with
unrestrained enthusiasm and defers to readers who alone can bestow
power by making a political decision to align themselves with it.

What can happen to that strangely paradoxical hail, now that *LERH* appears before you *in this book?* I think that identifying with Hunca Munca
now is a way of disavowing the possible devolution of *LERH* into the
equivalent of the police doll, of unperforming this book's call upon us to
array ourselves as subjects of its power. It is a paradox, of course; a paradox in which readers may participate—with what effects, I wonder?—in
2003, 2013, 2023. . . .

The explosion of CLS sociability, its strangely warlike and vulnerable par-
tial ascendency in law teaching, the absorption of many of its most distinctive ideas and agenda items (not to say, also, people) into the amoeba-
like rationality of the center, and the persistence of real critical work and
of the subtler, more evanescent social forms that sustain it—the present
republication of *LERH* will be the occasion for many people to connect
these dots into a story, tragic or comic, rising or falling, autobiographical
or "objective." If I had any influence on the resulting historical conversation, I would encourage people to make it "new" rather than "old" historicist—that is, genealogical rather than linear; baldly explicit about its own
involvement in making the past rather than funereal about a golden age
that may never have happened and that may not be over yet; present to it-

self as a fresh intervention; responsible about how it generates or narrows the opportunities for radical intellectual/political work.

NOTES

1. I wrote the first section of this essay in March–April 2003. Though I could have asked Duncan to explain many things to me about *LERH,* as I suggest below the answers would just have been "more text" for me to interpret. So I decided to read the pamphlet republished here as if he were completely unavailable to provide "the truth of the matter"—as indeed, in my view, he is. I don't think he would disagree. I have coaxed this essay in the direction of literary-critical engagement with the present legibility of a text marked very deeply by its presence in a present that is now past. I wrote the last two sections, however, in July 2003, after reading Duncan's draft Introduction and Afterword for this volume. Thanks to David Kennedy, Fernanda Nicola, and Judith Walcott for very helpful readings of various texts, including this one.

2. On Winstanley, see Gerrard Winstanley, *The Law of Freedom, and Other Writings,* ed. Christopher Hill (Cambridge and New York: Cambridge University Press, 1983); and Winstanley, *Selected Writings,* ed. Andrew Hopton (London: Aporia, 1989); Christopher Hill, *The Religion of Gerrard Winstanley* (Oxford: Past and Present Society, 1978).

3. The "kern" is the excess of recessed lead on either side of the raised letter on a piece of handset lead type. "To kern" is to reduce or increase the amount of this excess so that within words letters can be spaced equidistant from their mutual edges, rather than from their centers. Just for example: imagine the word *e x a m p l e* without kerning. Highbrow hand typesetting was kerned; lowbrow hand typesetting (like that used in the political tracts I am remembering) wasn't. Manual typewriting could not be kerned; the "l" got just as much space within a word as the "o." In the days just before we jumped to word-processing computers, I think, IBM Selectrics offered kerning and it was thought to be a huge advantage, even though some models held a whole line of type in memory and spat it onto the page in a distracting, error-prone sprint; our word-processing programs all now automatically kern. Type that is not kerned, especially when the space between letters is ample, emphasizes letters over words and makes us feel the work of construing the former into the latter; kerning somehow allows us to "gulp" whole words without noticing the letters that make them up. And in a world where everything is kerned, unkerned type signals "deliberately even aggressively lowbrow; mechanical, not electronic."

4. Christopher Hill, *Milton and the English Revolution* (New York: Viking Press, 1977).

5. Eric Hobsbawm and Terence Ranger, eds., *The Invention of Tradition* (New York: Cambridge University Press, 1992).

6. There is an outside chance that Duncan derived this name from a book published in 1983 by Claude Lévi-Strauss, *Le regard eloigné* (Librarie Plon, Paris: 1983); published in English, translated by Joachim Neugroshel and Phoebe Hoss, as *The View from Afar* (New York: Basic Books, 1984). But the dates are so close; perhaps the French version appeared so early in the year, and *LERH* so late, that this could be a source. If so, everything about Duncan's fascination with Lévi-Strauss's structuralism and about his spectatorial stance as an ethnographer are implied in the name of his fantastic press. If the dates are not friendly in this way, we would have to suppose that Duncan knew in advance the book's forthcoming status; possible, but unlikely. Note also that his monograph *The Rise and Fall of Classical Legal Thought* (1975, rpt. 1998) bears the imprint AFAR. (Thanks to Fernanda Nicola for providing these leads.)

7. A supposition bolstered by the copyright page, which provides: "(c) 1982, 1983 by Duncan Kennedy." Of course we are all "free" to try to retain copyright in work we publish with publishing houses; Afar, Inc., may have conceded copyright to Duncan. But Duncan's claim of copyright, without mention of the publisher, suggests that the house was and remains imaginary—that the only "real" thing about it is its name.

8. The use of the term *utopian* in the text is not a contradiction—Duncan's "utopian proposal" for curricular reform is not about establishing the ideal law school but about provoking a refusal by colleagues which they could not support without making ideological assertions.

9. Beatrix Potter, *The Tale of Two Bad Mice* (n.p., 1904). This is the original edition; Duncan was working from a 1908 reprint. For a delightful collection of Beatrix Potter tales, with wonderful reproductions, see *The Complete Tales of Beatrix Potter* (London: F. Warne & Co., 1989). For a readily accessible but visually somewhat inscrutable version, go to http://wiredforbooks.org/kids/beatrix/bm1.htm.

10. The literary-critical bibliography on the relationship between emblems and the written texts in which they appear is massive. The entry that most convinced me of the value of close reading of the sort I am about to perform is Edgar Wind, *Pagan Mysteries in the Renaissance* (Oxford: Oxford University Press, 1980).

11. Emphases are added; I will not note them as such again.

12. I asked several newcomers to *Two Bad Mice* whether they had the same reading experience, and they said they did.

13. Christopher Hill, *The World Turned Upside Down: Radical Ideas during the English Revolution* (New York: Penguin Books, 1975).

14. For the specifically seventeenth-century English elaborations of it, see Peter Stallybrass and Allon White, *The Politics and Poetics of Transgression* (Ithaca, NY: Cornell University Press, 1986).

15. From this point on, my essay was written in July 2003, after I'd read Duncan's Introduction and Afterword to this volume.

16. Now that I've read Duncan's Introduction and Afterword, I "know" that he "self-published" *LERH;* that the original allusion of AFAR may be to Lenin in Zurich, not Lévi-Strauss anywhere; and so on. Nuff said.

17. All three issues of *Lizard* bear the following notice on the first page: "Published by AFAR[;] disclaimer p. 3." And on page 3 of each issue appears the following notice: "*Lizard* is an emanation of a small faction within the critical legal studies movement, sometimes referred to as the True Left. *Lizard* does not in any way, official or unofficial, represent the views of the Conference on Critical Legal Studies. The contents of *Lizard* have not been discussed within CCLS, and it does not conform to the general attitude of the membership, which is far more responsible and boring than anything we would be interested in printing. Since most CLS people would dislike this paper were they to become familiar with it, it would be gross guilt by association to treat them as co-conspirators." The precise authorship and degree of collectivity that actually generated *Lizard* and its contents remain matters for speculation and private (coterie) "knowledge."

I have also seen a copy of the fugitive "Notes of an Oppositionist in Academic Politics." This really *is* typewritten and circulates only from hand to hand. It has a certain notoriety nevertheless: see Calvin Trillin, "A Reporter at Large: Harvard Law School," *New Yorker,* March 26, 1984, at 53, for one narrative of, and a moment in, its sociability.

18. *Webster's Third* defines *vain* this way: "1) having no real value, meaning or foundation: EMPTY, IDLE, WORTHLESS; 2) marked by futility or ineffectualness: FRUITLESS, UNSUCCESSFUL; 3) archaic: having or showing little sense or wisdom: FOOLISH, SILLY; 4) having or showing undue or excessive pride, esp. in one's appearance or achievements: CONCEITED." Philip Babcock Gove, ed., *Webster's Third New International Dictionary* (Springfield, MA: Merriam-Webster, Inc., 2002), p. 2528.

19. J. W. Saunders, "The Stigma of Print: A Note on the Social Bases of Tudor Poetry," *Essays in Criticism* 1 (1951), 139–64.

20. *Grutter v. Bollinger,* 123 S.Ct. 2325 (2003).

21. "Psycho-Social CLS: A Comment on the Cardozo Symposium," 6 *Cardozo L. Rev.* 1013 (1985); reprinted in Duncan Kennedy, *Essays on Legal Education* (n.p.: n.p., 1996).

Afterword

Duncan Kennedy

This Afterword is intended as a contribution to an imaginary archive of radical thinking about law, the context for *Legal Education and the Reproduction of Hierarchy* (*LERH*). It includes notes on the author (me), on Critical Legal Studies in 1983, on the publishing history of *LERH* and the hidden meaning of its form, a remark on "radicalism" as it figures in *LERH*, a few words on the current status of legal hierarchy (it's doing better than ever), and an account of what happened to CLS after 1983. The pieces can be read separately, according to taste.

The Author

I graduated from Yale Law School in 1970, having participated in a small-scale collective student project of institutional reform, coupled with attempts at analysis of how our legal education fit into the larger picture of the politics of the moment. The politics included the war in Vietnam, the disintegration of the civil rights movement, the failure of the War on Poverty, and the first stirrings of second-wave feminism. It was radicalizing for many of us.

After a year clerking on the U.S. Supreme Court, I started teaching at Harvard Law School in the fall of 1971, and got tenure in 1976. By 1981, when I wrote *LERH*, I had taught Contracts for five years and Torts for four, in classes of about 140 (as well as Legal Process for a year, Trusts for two years, and a course on the History of Legal Thought for eight). I had spent the academic year 1980–81 working as a paralegal (I am not a member of the bar) at the then brand-new Legal Services Institute (now the

Hale and Dorr Legal Services Center) in Jamaica Plain, Boston, and teaching a course there for students doing an experimental one-year full-time program of preparation for legal services practice. Aside from a student summer at Debevoise, Plympton, Lyons and Gates in 1969, I had no law practice experience.

During the seventies, I participated in the general "softening" of the traditional Socratic method in large law school classes. I worked, along with a fluctuating group of about ten colleagues, on internal law school reform issues, including reducing first-year class size, pass/fail in the first year, and the "no-hassle pass"; expanding clinical opportunities, a liberal policy of promotion to tenure, affirmative action for women and African Americans in entry-level faculty appointments, and introducing more race- and gender-oriented material into the curriculum. We also tried self-consciously to inflect the growth of the faculty away from what we saw as intellectually mediocre mainstream appointments toward people doing left (and occasionally right) innovative work. These activities involved collaboration with law students in a sixties-influenced mode of strategizing and acting together that violated conventional ideas about the proper boundaries between faculty and students.

Starting in 1976, I participated in what we called the Marx Study Group (not the *Marxist* study group), organized by Karl Klare, which had a core group of six male and female lawyers and academics. We read and passionately discussed a good deal of Marx's work and that of the "critical" or Western European Marxist current of the twentieth century. In 1980, I helped organize a short-lived venture self-mockingly called the League of Left Study Groups, consisting of about forty Harvard law students interested in the rich left-wing theoretical writing that was then a feature of the American intellectual scene, and in the brand new legal literature that we had begun to produce in the late 1970s in the context of Critical Legal Studies.

Critical Legal Studies in 1983

Along with law students in general, the intended audience for *LERH* was the group of younger legal academics who participated in the Conference on Critical Legal Studies. CLS began at a conference at the University of Wisconsin Law School in Madison in 1977. The idea of the conference, as David Trubek and I initially conceived it, was to explore the possibility of an alliance between "law and society" scholars and a younger group of more assertively leftist legal academics and soon-to-be academics. These included participants in the activist moment at the Yale Law School that I mentioned above, several of whom had by then gotten tenure at law schools here and there, the Marx Study Group people, the new group of Harvard professors and their recently graduated left students, and a scattering of New Leftists who had up to then been isolated in their institutions.

The idea of an alliance with the law-and-society scholars was short-lived, but the "rump" consolidated, and over the next fifteen years CLS members from different law schools volunteered to organize a dozen large conferences (one hundred to seven hundred participants) and ten or so "summer camps" in which groups of ten to twenty spent from a few days to a week studying and discussing left legal and general social theoretical literature together.

The conference turned out to be an idea whose time was then. Growth occurred as people who had been out there all along "discovered" CLS, as students of the CLS core group went into law teaching, and as people entering law teaching with a generally progressive orientation looked around to find who in their new discipline they could affiliate with. The big conferences were intense, energized by the continuing political interaction of the expanding group of regulars, a fluctuating group of law professors who were curious about what was going on, students at the host institution, and students who traveled from other schools where they had been engaged by one of the crit regulars. The summer camps, with a sampling of the same personnel in an intimate setting for a longer time, were even more intense.

I've been asked a million times why CLS "failed," but it seems a more interesting question how such an overtly leftist, anti-mainstream academic movement, with no outside funding of any kind, could take off, expand so quickly, and last for about fifteen years as a highly visible factor in legal academia (of all places). I'll have a shot at explaining the downside as an afterword to this Afterword. Here's an account of the upside, the milieu at which *LERH* was aimed.

CLS came into existence in the full swing of one of the most dramatic moments of change in the history of U.S. legal education.[1] Between 1970 and 1990, the number of ABA-accredited law schools expanded from 146 to 175; the number of law students at those schools, from 82,041 to 135,518. Between 1975 and 1990, the number of women students grew from 7,031 to 55,818, which was from 8.5 percent to 42.1 percent. Between 1975 and 1990, the number of students of color grew from 8,712 (7.8 percent) to 17,330 (13.6 percent).

More important for CLS as an organization, the number of full-time faculty grew steadily over the whole period between 1970 and 1990, from 2,873 to 5,366, and then leveled off. Between 1975 and 1990, the number of full-time women faculty rose from 517 to 1,338, and then leveled off. From 1985 (first year with figures) to 1990, the number of full-time minority teachers rose from 301 to 512. These developments created an opportunity, just because there were so many people entering the system without preconceptions about how it was and had always been organized. By 1990, the wave of change had passed: the system was growing slowly, if at all, and almost everyone in it had been exposed to or heard about CLS and decided on an attitude toward it. Whereas the average age of law teachers must have plummeted in the late seventies and eighties, it must have begun to rise again, rapidly, after 1990.

The growth in the number of law teachers occurred through entry-level recruitment, by and large, of people who were in their late twenties and early thirties. The opening of this large market coincided with the collapse of the market for PhDs in the humanities and the social sciences. Many people who might have chosen English or history or sociology or political science as an academic career ended up in law instead. For many of them, the next best thing to being an academic in the humanities or social sciences was to enter the real world and pursue social justice through law.

But faith in the possibility of transforming American society through civil rights litigation was beginning to wane around 1980. The Warren Court had made it seem that constitutional law was intrinsically on the side of the weak and the oppressed; the Burger Court was slowly but steadily undoing that sense. The Democratic Party had begun its long opportunist slide to the right. Reagan was elected in 1980, shadowing the dream that if one couldn't be a civil rights litigator, one could be a progressive government lawyer.

Some detracked graduate students and would-be civil rights lawyers had studied in leftist undergraduate programs in the late sixties and seventies, and perhaps tried a master's program for a year or two. Many had been activists or counterculturalists of one kind or another and/or had been exposed to critical theory in the humanities or social sciences in one of its myriad American forms of the 1970s. They were baby boomers, born after 1947, and a significant minority of them were New Left baby boomers, arriving on the teaching market for law schools starting around 1977 (and gone from the teaching market by the early 1990s).

Feminism was developing fast, branching out into liberal, cultural, socialist, and radical variants. The small numbers of women on law faculties were willy-nilly players in local gender politics, and they had an audience as law reformers and academic writers. After the unutterable downer of the disintegration of the civil rights movement around 1970 and the descent of the northern urban ghettos into a kind of hell, there were new possibilities as African Americans and other minorities of color entered all kinds of middle-class and intelligentsia job markets.

Law teaching seemed to offer a way out of the impasse—it allowed activist engagement without having to be a full-time lawyer and a milieu that was intellectually exciting and increasingly politicized, without the disciplinary fetishes of the Ph.D. world. It was rare for a faculty to require more than one published article for tenure, and the article was typically published in a student-edited (not peer-reviewed) journal. The number of such journals increased even faster than the number of schools, from 374 in 1975 to 569 in 1990, with the emphasis on "law and . . . " publications tailored to the output of the younger academic generation.

The intellectual poverty of mainstream legal education created an opportunity, with risks. Quite apart from the complete ignorance of critical theory, there was a general atheoretical, or more commonly anti-theoretical, attitude among the influentials on most law faculties, and among the mass of professors on all faculties. Those who did see themselves as theoretical, and were sometimes powerful though few in number, were likely to be sharply hostile to any form of theory that emerged on their left. They were basically the older legal-process intellectuals, the older law-and-society intellectuals, the founders of law and economics, and the new generation of liberal constitutional rights theorists, who were only a few years older than the crits, much in rebellion against legal process, dismissive of law and society, and ambivalent about law and economics. Ronald Dworkin was their figurehead. They were the opposite of countercultural and the furthest possible thing from critical theory.

Don't forget the brilliance of the CLS scholarship and the creativity of the organizing strategy, which eschewed both formal organizational structure and the development of any kind of CLS program or manifesto but nonetheless managed to avoid being co-opted by the smug liberal elitists or destroyed by the authoritarians and random crazies who are drawn like flies to honey by apparently unboundaried left ventures.

CLS events of this golden age had an over-the-top quality without (usually) being over the edge, and what was more, we tried to "process" what happened, subjectively, confrontively, rather than living in denial and bureaucracy. We had some good speakers, too; charisma spread through the ranks (for a sample of one style, see Peter Gabel's piece, above). There was a strong anti-elitist internal ethos, aimed against status differences based on what law school you taught at, or for that matter studied at, and an ethic of support for beginning scholars from veteran scholars.

But perhaps just as or more important was that many law schools at all levels of the law school pecking order permitted virtually unlimited long-distance telephone calls and virtually unlimited reproduction of documents. Most schools would pay for a trip to an academic conference if you were "giving a paper" (one of the origins, along with egalitarianism, of the CLS conference mode, in which there were two hundred attendees and one hundred papers). Law school deans not uncommonly saw CLS events at their schools as a plus in the scramble for reputation.

The white male lefties who set out to take advantage of the opportunity were drawn from two main sources. There were post-Marxists, disillusioned by the decline of the student left of the 1960s into many kinds of sectarianism, often including fanatic adherence to some form of "materialism" or "base/superstructure" thinking. And there were postliberals, equally disillusioned, but with a completely different group: the liberal leaders of the war in Vietnam, the liberal equivocators who let the ghettoes burn and the Black Panthers die in police ambushes, the liberal labor leaders who watched the labor movement go down the tubes, and the liberal patriarchs who loved to promote women who made them feel good as guys. We were countercultural, but generally cautiously so. We were into ultraradical theory, but mainly in the mode of excavating and then cherry-picking bodies of ideas to which we felt we'd been denied access by the homogenized Cold War modes of 1950s and early 1960s elite education. And we were aesthetic modernists, by and large.

I venture that an issue for many of us was shame or abjection, not around the question "What did you do in the war?" but around the question "What were you doing when your contemporaries were getting arrested in Mississippi or Oakland?" There was also the insistence of both liberal activists and Marxist and post-Marxist and black radical activists that theory was bullshit and academic or school politics was bullshit squared; that the only real politics was some form of state-oriented politics or some kind of community organizing. White men in particular could be radicals only in so much as they somehow managed to act both on behalf of and in full subordination to some group, of which they were not members, that was "really" suffering.

In the various attempts to reconstruct the politics of the time, it is sometimes said that we were Marxists and therefore preoccupied with class at the expense of race and gender issues, and that this explains the demise of the movement. This is pretty far off. One of the main reasons the post-Marxists were "post" was that the people who were proprietary about Marxism thought economy + class was the one and only key, and the CLS people did not. They were, along with the postliberals, very much preoccupied with race, and a large part of the foundational CLS scholarship of Alan Freeman, Mark Tushnet, and Karl Klare was on race issues. This was also the moment when Richard Delgado was inviting the white liberal constitutionalists *not* to write about race.

White feminists were part of the scene from the beginning, since their numbers in legal academia had begun to increase in the mid-1970s, and some of them were crits and some were not, not at all, thank you. It was obvious that CLS conference programs should devote sessions to race and gender, more sessions than to labor law, but it was also the case that the central project was, first, "theory," and, second, aimed at developing a position about and within law that would be just plain left, rather than an African American left or a feminist left position.

Before moving on to the publishing history of *LERH,* it is worth noting that in 1983 what we now call identity politics was barely coming into existence, that there was no American postmodernism anywhere in the vicinity of the legal academy, and that the "linguistic turn" was barely beginning in what was not yet called just "theory." Boomer leftists were just beginning to have children and renew their religious roots, but the turn to domesticity was not yet. Married crits with children didn't hesitate, whether they were mothers or fathers, to commit to one-week summer camps and smoke dope.

Publishing History

In 1981, David Kairys came up with the idea of a joint project between the National Lawyers' Guild's Theoretical Studies Committee and the Conference on Critical Legal Studies. He proposed to edit a collection of radical writings about law, to be published by Andre Shiffrin, then head of the

New Press (soon to be acquired by Pantheon). The conference had only the most minimal existence, and a constant internal argument went on about whether we should have officers and elections or continue with the wholly informal arrangement in which Mark Tushnet was the "Secretary," in charge of the mailing list and the bank account, with no rules at all. It turned out that the book project, somewhat to David's disappointment, didn't oblige the conference people to adopt a formal organization, because we were all (as I remember) more than willing to delegate to him full responsibility for everything. He asked me to write a chapter about legal education.

In July 1981, in a spurt over about three weeks, I wrote just about all of the pamphlet you have before you. I revised it a bit and submitted it at the beginning of September 1981, but of course it was too long, so we agreed that the book, *The Politics of Law*, would include chapters 1, 2, 5, and 6 only. The book appeared in 1982; there was a second edition in 1990; and a third, for which I somewhat revised my chapter, in 1998. I submitted the manuscript to the *Journal of Legal Education*, and they published a short version in 1982 shortly after the book came out.

In the winter of 1982–83, I decided to self-publish the full manuscript, more or less exactly as it was in September 1981, as a pamphlet. I was reading lots of books about revolutionary movements at the time, trying to figure out how they worked before they became oppressive governments, and so was exposed to pamphlet literature as an idea. Through an Office of Information Technology, Harvard Law School was for the first time making word processing available to its faculty. I was influenced by the cult of the handmade artifact, in which I was indoctrinated at Shady Hill School in Cambridge in the 1950s, and by the ideology of the pamphlet itself, my own ideology of the time, affirming the desirability and possibility of the "revolution of civil society," carried out without official media, "interstitially" rather than from above or below the institutions where we work.

I think I paid about $3 per copy for one hundred copies (it would cost less per copy when I got up my courage to order larger lots). I sent it in boxes to the Conference on Critical Legal Studies held at Georgetown University Law Center in March 1981, for free distribution. But—bummer—it didn't get there in time for display at the registration desk. In the end, only about fifty copies were picked up, and I had to pay to ship the other fifty back to Cambridge. The Harvard Book Store in Cambridge sold pamphlets, in the grand tradition of left-wing bookstores. They put it on display, with a small markup, and it almost immediately began to sell steadily, if modestly. After that, self-publication was pure pleasure.

A Reading of the Form of the Pamphlet

The IBM Selectric was the state-of-the-art typewriter of the time. It allowed accurate correction of typos and produced copy that was much better looking than what had preceded it. But unless you got a special ball, it had only one type face, twelve point Courier, and, of course, you couldn't use italics or righthand justify. This meant that, for people who wrote things, there was an enormous difference between the look of even the most professionally produced "manuscript," more properly "typescript," and something actually *in print*. Once you had a typed manuscript, by 1981 you Xeroxed it (rather than having to mimeograph it), and it was often possible to find free Xeroxing because copiers were multiplying in office bays.

Here is my reading of the "artifact," opportunistically combining what I remember I intended with other people's interpretations and my own search, after it was out, for unintended or maybe unconscious meanings in it. The pamphlet tells us that it is an artifact because it is much more *in print* than a typed manuscript, while definitely not appearing to have been commercially produced. *LERH* was accordingly square, 7" x 7", so that it could be made of 8 ½" x 14" (legal-size) sheets folded in half and then cropped. Each 14" x 7" sheet had two side-by-side pages on each side, which had to be numbered so that when they were stacked up, saddle-stitched (stapled through the middle), and folded, they read in sequence. A square bound back would have cost a lot more and suggested publication, sale on bookstore shelves, and placement in libraries, rather than distribution in the street. The original was photocopied, as opposed to typeset and printed, using another new technology that was cheap and produced a look that was, again, betwixt and between Xeroxing and *in print*.

The front and back covers are hand-lettered, using Letraset stick-on letters and graph paper, with minimal adjustment of letter size to space, just as Janet Halley observed. The cover looks a little like the layout of pre–World War I French socialist poster art and a little like Mao's "Little Red Book," in the mode of self-mockery. The Broadway typeface contradicts the Commie red. My name in Times New Roman is a reassuring gesture. AFAR might mean that the author is coming from a place that is a long way from "the mainstream," as in Janet Halley's reading, and it might be a reference to Lenin's "Letters from Afar," written in Switzerland before the Germans sent him back to St. Petersburg in a sealed train to screw up the Russian war effort, a stay abroad brilliantly described by Alexander Solzhenitsyn in his *Lenin in Zurich*[2] (found in the author's library with date 1980 in his handwriting on the flyleaf). But another possibility is an acronym like those of the guerilla groups that multiplied in Latin America in the sixties and seventies (e.g., the FARC): perhaps "Armed Forces of Anarchist Revolution" or more consistent with the text, "American Front for Anarchist Resistance."

The typescript was turned into an original for photocopying in the Information Technology Office, with patience and humor, by one D— G—, who seemed to enjoy diverting Harvard's resources in an unexpected way. It is in twelve point Courier, to give a typewritten look, and uses underlining, though italics were available. But it is righthand justified and the word processor fits the letters together, as Janet Halley points out, instead of giving each letter, whether *i* or *m*, the same amount of space, again placing the pamphlet halfway between typed and *in print*. The back cover represents visually the argument that hierarchy in advanced welfare corporate capitalism is diamond-shaped rather than pyramidal. (See page 000.) The endpapers are a picture of Saturn in a hand-drawn black circle representing outer space. As Halley suggests, this reads like "from outer space," and goes with AFAR, or "spaceshot," but Saturn with its rings is also mysterious and diffusely symbolic. *Saturnine* means "stubborn."

Janet Halley's account of the illustrations from Beatrix Potter's *The Tale of Two Bad Mice* is perfect. I would add only that the two illustrations suggest the two dimensions of critical post-Marxist thinking about domination. In the first illustration, the threat is death by the material, violent means of the mousetrap, representing the use of physical force to sustain the status quo (not "state force to sustain capitalism"; see page 000). It amused me that the job of explaining how this works falls to the father, with the mother as spectator and the children alarmed. In the second illustration, the mother is allocated the task of explaining that what looks like a "real" policeman is only a doll, and the older children have already slipped by him to peek in the window of the dollhouse. Although *LERH* is Gramscian in inspiration, the picture suggests the Althusserian theory of interpellation in *Ideology and the Ideological State Apparatuses (Notes toward an Investigation),*[3] in which the policeman constitutes the citizen by yelling "Hey, you" at him, and resistance is in the mind rather than on the picket line. *LERH* might be understood as an attempt to continue the symbolic work of the mother.

The mice live in a cozy burrow in the wall of the little girl's very bourgeois establishment, and they forage. The whole thing evokes (for me) a very different relationship to the class system than the complete rejection and outsideness that was boringly claimed in the radical milieus of the time. The mice are modeling a relationship of parasitism, subversion, and appreciation of the finer aspects of bourgeois living, and even of bourgeois art as represented by Ms. Potter herself, while keeping in touch with their inner rage and sustaining a counterhegemonic enclave. (See page 137.)

The page layout of the body of the text is unusual. The square format produces, when you open the pamphlet, a 14" wide, 7" high double page. The large bottom margin, along with narrow side margins, with page numbers in the running head, accentuates the effect, producing a block of text that is 4 ¾" high but 11 ½" inches wide. The whole evokes (for me) the horizontal, long and low "strip" effect that is so important in modernist residential and commercial and industrial architecture, furniture, cars, and appliances—all in opposition to the vertical look of "classical" design.

Does all this have a "political subtext?" Perhaps that *LERH* combines two rebellious, avant-garde strands from the pre–World War II period, the leftist and the modernist, without subordinating one to the other.

"Radicalism" in LERH

I use the term *radical* often in the pamphlet. In 1981, an important aspect of the world of academia in general, and of big cities and small university towns, was that there was a radical identity, a political rather than a cultural or racial identity. It was partly negative, grouping people who didn't believe that the established politicians, social and political commentators, and academics who defined themselves as liberals against conservatives were serious enough about change to merit allegiance.

The sixties had discredited the liberals' traditional social program (labor unionization, public housing, the welfare system, supplemented by the compromised and ultimately failed War on Poverty and by the compromised and ultimately stalled push for a colorblind version of civil rights). The same for their international program, which, as we saw it, was the Cold War "containment" alliance with right-wing regimes everywhere, culminating in the Vietnam War, which became more rather than less murderous as the Soviet threat faded after 1968.

There was no single positive radical programmatic idea, and the continued existence of this tendency was already very much in question as the "preppie look" caught on, signaling the cultural counterrevolution. Radicals might turn out to be orthodox Marxists, counterculturally inclined anarchists, social Catholics, radical feminists, black nationalists, or people who rejected all of the above but were interested in any kind of initiative that might shake up the seemingly stalemated "system."

There were still organizations whose members thought of themselves as animated by radical politics in this sense, and their ideologies were what produced the internal life and conflict and evolution of organizations that were devoted to such causes as labor, pacifism, the environment, grassroots community organizing, feminism, and legal services for the poor. There were "tendencies" within feminism—liberal feminism versus socialist feminism—or among environmentalists—Greenpeace direct-action people versus liberal incremental litigators. African Americans who were politically active were quite deeply split between those who identified with the integrationist "civil rights establishment" and those who were more or less "race conscious," or for that matter separatist or black nationalist or direct-action oriented; more or less willing to work with white people; and so forth. One could live a full life following and participating in these internecine battles.

The liberals were immensely more powerful and more "established" everywhere than they are now. It still seemed plausible that the agenda was to drive them to the left, while swelling our ranks with theirs. They were losing, however, not to the left, which had destroyed itself in McGovern ineffectualness or Black Panther and Weather Underground failed terrorism or party-building delusions, but to the resurgent right represented by the Richard Nixons and the Ronald Reagans. The liberals were, accordingly, solely and obsessively preoccupied with the question of how much of their historic program they had to give up—just surrender or repeal or roll back—in order to retain enough votes to stay in power. The liberal establishment in the media, academia, and the legal profession was as worried about this as the politicians themselves, because the liberals overwhelmingly believed in the liberal welfare regulatory state as the main vehicle through which good could be done in the world.

Many students who did not, would never have called themselves radicals situated themselves between radicals and liberals, picking and choosing among the positions of the two sides according to the issue. *LERH* was an appeal to liberal students and in-between students to move to the left, as well as an appeal to radical students to grope forward in a particular direction. It was just as much an appeal to the generation of boomer activists just then entering legal academia as assistant professors to adopt a radical attitude within their institutions. As the right got stronger and the liberals gave more and more ground, it seemed feasible to try to define an alternative—radical, egalitarian, and anarchist, with a dose of "premature postmodernism" in the argument that power is productive of hierarchical selves, rather than merely repressive.

We were looking to form a new minority, rather than the new majority the liberals were desperately seeking—a minority that would renounce state power and do what we self-mockingly called "the Long March through the Institutions" (by analogy to Mao's Long March through the countryside when the forces of Chiang Kai-shek defeated the Chinese Communists in the cities). The single most provocative thing about *LERH*, it turned out, even more provocative than "equal pay for janitors," was the insistence that it was not meaningless to "resist" even at "bourgeois dinner parties," and by obvious extension in legal education and large corporate law firms.

The Current Situation

The system described in *LERH* has gotten tighter in the ensuing twenty years,[4] and mainstream scholarship on the legal profession now acknowledges things that only mavericks like Rick Abel[5] and Carrie Menkel-Meadow[6] used to talk about. The bar is even more highly stratified than it used to be, with greater differences in incomes but also in the organization of firms and in the class origins and current prestige of practitioners. The system rigidly determines a place for everyone and everyone in his or her place. If it is her place, then keep in mind the recent study that showed that law firms with lots of women partners pay their women associates better than firms with overwhelmingly male partners,[7] and you might mention that to the partner at the firm dinner when he puts his hand on your leg under the table. African Americans don't make partner, or not much.[8]

Behind the hierarchy of law firms, there is the feeder system of the hierarchy of law schools. As one researcher recently put it, "the identity of the institution from which a graduate receives the J.D. degree may be the single most important factor in the graduate's career path."[9] Average student indebtedness has increased to an amount well over $85,000 for the maybe 80 percent of law students who borrow.[10] Job security for associates has gone out the window as their first-year compensation has increased, so the chances that you will be let go or that your firm will go under or merge into an entity that no longer needs you are way up, and the chances that you will end up a partner in your first employer are way down.[11]

Radicalism does *not* mean believing that by forming law student study groups you can abolish this system. It does mean finding some way to rebel in law school, maybe starting from the description of Third World Coalitions and law review reform struggles that Harris and Maeda provide in their chapter above. It means recognizing the system for what it is when, all around you, your fellow lawyers are denying that it exists or glorying in what they happen to be getting out of it at the moment. It means rejecting it as both unjust and socially unnecessary. It means trying to locate other people who feel the same way, without getting yourself fired. It means looking for small enactments of rejection and resistance that affirm that one is a person of moral substance. And it means looking for the targets of opportunity that might allow building a minoritarian alliance over time that could sustain itself. After graduation, it seems to me to mean first of all trying to find a morally tolerable law firm to work for, or to move to from whatever firm one is forced into working for by the status degradation ritual of the law school placement process.

What Happened to Critical Legal Studies

What happened to Critical Legal Studies may not be of much interest if you are a law student. It does seem to intrigue quite a few legal academics. There are two narratives about what happened. The first is the narrative of organizational expansion and disintegration, and of disaffiliation. The second is that of the survival of CLS as a body of literature, as a "school" of legal thought still producing through "successor networks," and as a pervasive influence on legal scholarship not just in the United States but worldwide. When we left the story a few pages ago, what was happening was the flooding into CLS of white women law teachers (American and

Canadian) and African American and other law teachers of color, both men and women. There also arrived a new generation of white men, much more graduate student–like than their predecessors (who were now dubbed the "old white male heavies").

It would be wrong to homogenize the newcomers under the rubric of identity politics, although that was an important element. The white women and African Americans were highly various politically and theoretically, and they were as much in conflict among themselves as with the old white male heavies. The younger white men were postmodernist, either in a leftist Foucaldian mode or in a dandified, defiantly politically incorrect Derridean mode. There was an initial alliance of the po-mo young with white women and minorities against the frumpy universalist phallocentrism of the old white male heavies. It was not to endure.

The combination of generational, gender, racial, and theory agendas of contradictory kinds produced what was, for me, the most exciting and fertile moment of intellectual, political, and intimate social life that I've experienced. What was great about it for many of us was that it was the first time in our lives that we engaged our "others," whoever they might be, in very straight talk about the dynamics of power that existed, not just in the society writ large but in the smallest social interactions. This straight talk was in a context of commitment and hope for a transformation of our common professional space, and it included not just frankness but also commitment to talking through rage toward reconciliation.

There are many reasons why it was short-lived. The context was the one well described by Pierre Bourdieu in "The Academic Field."[12] Each of us was not only a group member but also an entrepreneur on the ladder of academic jobs. Some of us were tenured, with our chances of lateral movement hostage to CLS; and some of us were untenured, with our tenure hostage to CLS. Some of us were beneficiaries of affirmative action, and some of us of negative action. CLS might be one's only chance to get on the map, but once there, one might be stuck or destroyed as a result. No one was accountable for the microdecisions that determined what CLS looked like to the mainstream that controlled tenure and lateral hires. This was particularly true after the national media decided that Harvard Law School was a "story," the story of sixties radicals reemerging with tenure to disrupt everything good and true.

CLS was partly destroyed by repression. One can get a sense of how time changes all things by contrasting Paul Carrington's famous call for CLS professors to "depart the academy," because they were morally unsuited to teach law,[13] with his piece in this volume. He was the dean of Duke Law School at the time. A bunch of assistant professors associated (in reality or in the eyes of their colleagues) with CLS were denied tenure, in circumstances suggesting that they would have gotten tenure without the association. There was a none-too-subtle attempt by a number of entry-level hiring interviewers to get a sense from applicants of whether they were "sound," meaning hostile to CLS. And a great deal of really silly, but intimidating, red-baiting nonsense was written about CLS by people who knew better.[14]

Given this setting, it is fanciful to imagine that the "question that killed critical legal studies" was: So, what's your alternative vision?[15] The refusal to formulate an alternative vision was what allowed CLS to exist as a "location" for exhilarating encounters.[16] Along with the ethical tensions of entrepreneurship and repression, what happened was that the participants in the cross-generational, cross-racial, cross-gender discussion came to find it unbearable.

It was partly a matter of substantive disagreements about things like the CLS critique of rights; or the relative importance of developing a specifically legal kind of critical theory versus the effort to develop new theories of how race or gender worked themselves out through law; or the implications, constructive or destructive, of "fancy" theory for law reform work.

It was also partly a matter of the substance in style. Cultural and radical feminists who were interested in coalitions with white men were also committed to confronting them very hard about their whole gendered mode of being, and minorities were no less committed to getting the issues of unconscious racism and silencing on the table. The old white male heavies were no less committed to avoiding what many of them saw as the worst aspect of seventies leftism: the tendency of nonsectarian white male radicals to just shut up and take race and gender denunciation without daring to talk back. The whole idea of "process orientation" was to surface this kind of conflict. It was often very painful for all concerned, partly because everyone felt that CLS should be a "refuge," and everyone got mad that it wasn't.

A second divisive emotional structure had to do with theory needs— the "anxiety of influence" of the newcomers and the "anxiety of proprietorship" of old-timers. For many of the white women and minority profs interested in CLS, it was an important article of faith that women and minorities had a specific intellectual contribution to make. The alternative to assimilation into the mainstream was to assert that there were specific failings of white male scholarship in general, including that of the left and right margins of the mainstream. One failing was the "neglect" of gender and minority issues. Nonassimilating women and minorities set out to write about "their" issues and had a relatively unproblematic open space to move into.

Both for radical and cultural feminists and for minority scholars, there was another necessary claim—that they had a different methodology, a different kind of theory. They wanted to operate not just on neglected subject matters but also with tools that were their own rather than those that had built the white male master's house. This claim was endlessly and interestingly problematic. It could have a wide variety of proposed contents, ranging from the claims for "narrative" as the essence of outsider jurisprudence, to the assertion that there is a "black point of view" or a "woman's point of view" that white men "just don't get," all the way to the claim that advanced postmodern theoretical techniques, inaccessible to the vast majority of white male law professors (though of course wholly the invention of dead white male European non–law professors) were necessary to capture minority or women's experience.

The younger pomo guys had their own theory narrative, in which the old white male heavies were what Italians call *vecchio* Marxists, essentializers in lots of different ways. Their need to be theoretically new was just as intense, in the oedipal mode, as that of the feminists and minorities. And came up just as sharply against the need of the old white male heavies to understand themselves as the proprietors of a radically new, anti-mainstream critical theory of law that anticipated just about any idea that a feminist, a race-conscious minority professor, or a smart-ass pomo kid thought they'd come up with on their own. Of course, many of us on all sides struggled against this emotional dead end. Kim Crenshaw, Mary Joe Frug, and I pushed for a coalition concept, with only limited success.

The modes of disaffiliation were various. Many of the first generation of white males were tentative to begin with. They simply faded away. Many of the first generation who participated enthusiastically into the mid-1980s dropped out because of the opening up of new opportunities in the mainstream and their reaction against the combination of process orientation and dramatic identity and generational politics. For the young pomos, the failure of alliance with either white feminists or African Americans and the disgruntlement of sonship led in the same direction. There must be fifty tenured profs around the country at more or less prestigious schools who would be unlikely to mention that CLS was the formative moment of their academic youth, almost like having been, however briefly, a Communist in the 1930s.

African American along with Latino/a and Asian American law teachers formed the Critical Race Theory network, beginning at a meeting in Madison in 1989. This network combined people who were aiming to create a minority organization that would participate in CLS as a coalition partner with left-of-liberal white men and white feminists, those looking to create a milieu for a distinctively minority "outsider" scholarship, and those looking to create an ideologically moderate "safe space" within which to work on how to deal with the white faculties where they experienced themselves as tokens, but tokens facing tenure writing requirements that were getting stiffer every year. Safe space seemed to win out, and Critical Race Theory split along ethnic lines. It remained a name for a style of scholarship rather than a movement. Only the LatCrits continue to hold big, multidimensional conferences at regular intervals and keep theoretical and practical concerns in fruitful tension.

Nothing like Critical Race Theory came into existence for feminist law professors interested in theory, not because they already had the Women in the Law Conference but because, at the same moment when many of them were becoming fed up with the old white male heavies, they were bitterly and permanently split by the anti-pornography campaign. Feminist legal theory is an umbrella term for a wildly diverse, far-ranging set of approaches, sharply challenged on one side by black feminist scholarship and on the other by queer legal theory.

By 1992, it was clear that the "movement" had become "just another academic conference," as Mark Tushnet put it at the Crit Networks Conference, a coalition event of CLS, Critical Race Theory and the "femcrits," held that year at Harvard and Northeastern Law Schools. It was a place for young scholars to present their left-wing or, more specifically, CLS-influenced work to a still very substantial audience. But it had fragmented in terms of theory into a half dozen approaches, and the approaches were no longer confronting each other. The idea that the strong emotions released in a big or small meeting would have to be processed in a self-conscious, psychologically sophisticated way so that the movement could continue to grow and advance seemed utterly of the past. Likewise the idea that radical law professors should organize permanent challenges, school by school, to the reproduction of legal hierarchy. People were more concerned with keeping bitter disagreements and conflicting views of the history from surfacing and disrupting the diffuse good vibes than they were with yet another hashing out of disagreements that seemed insurmountable. Legal education had reequilibrated.

Before moving on, I note without regret that the above account is no more neutral or merely factual than any of the other attempts at histories of CLS.

What's Left

There are several hundred CLS-inspired articles on just about every area of law. They are the main existing alternative to the mainstream liberal and right-wing libertarian stuff that fills the reviews. This literature is still expanding, slowly but steadily, because CLS is still very much alive as a "school." CLS literature is also expanding because there are two successor networks: INTELL,[17] which focuses on labor law worldwide, and the European Law Research Center,[18] which focuses on international law, comparative law, and law and development. Recognizably "crittish" literature continues to appear for another reason: academics who have never met a crit in their life read the canonical works of the movement and set out to contribute. Many crit ideas, and particularly the notion of the "indeterminacy" of both classical legal analysis and of policy analysis, have become part of American legal academic common sense. Much of the institutional agenda of CLS has been adopted, little by little, by law schools at all levels of the status hierarchy.

The white women and minorities and rebellious young, and most of the old white male heavies, have made their peace, joining the diffuse liberal to left-liberal alliance that confronts a similarly diffuse conservative alliance in legal education. It would not be too much to say that CLS succeeded, against the odds, in politicizing legal theory and legal education, while failing, according to the odds, to radicalize either.

There are CLS critiques of most of the modes of the mainstream, and a particularly elaborate critique of law and economics. The CLS critique of rights remains alive and influential and is the most galling for liberals and identity-politics devotees. But there are also critiques of mainstream law and society thinking, of depoliticized versions of postmodernism, and of liberal and radical feminist legal theory. Of course, a good number of the authors of these critiques might disavow them today. For unreconstructed crits like myself, they remain powerful, interesting, and too soon abandoned.

A striking aspect of all this is that it is international. Globalization, as Ugo Mattei and Anna di Robilant point out,[19] creates a global market for American law and a global market for modes of resistance to American law, of which CLS is one. There has been a British Critical Legal Studies network for almost as long as there has been an American one, combining Marxist and postmodern tendencies, and a Continental European one likewise, and now there is a South African one. There is no American organization with which they can have uneasy diplomatic relations, and there is nothing like a sense of a common transnational line. But the sun never sets on Critical Legal Studies.

The upshot is that there is a lot of radical legal scholarship and scholarly activity still around for the student who is willing to look for it, even if there is not the sense of an all-inclusive, open movement to join or rebel against. It's time for something new here, too.

NOTES

1. All the statistics that follow are from Carl Auerbach, *Historical Statistics of Legal Education* (Chicago: American Bar Foundation, 1997). Thanks to Alejandra Nunez for research help.

2. Alexander Solzhenitsyn, *Lenin in Zurich: Chapters* (trans. H. T. Willetts, New York: Farrar, Straus & Giroux, 1976).

3. Louis Althusser, *Lenin and Philosophy, and Other Essays*, trans. Ben Brewster (New York: Monthly Review Press, 2001).

4. See John P. Heinz, Robert L. Nelson, Edward O. Laumann, and Ethan Michelson, *The Changing Character of Lawyers' Work: Chicago in 1975 and 1995*, 32 Law & Soc. Rev. 751 (1998).

5. Richard Abel, *American Lawyers* (New York: Oxford University Press, 1989).

6. Carrie Menkel-Meadow, *Portia in a Different Voice: Speculations on a Women's Lawyering Process*, 1 Berkeley Women's L.J. 39 (1985).

7. Elizabeth Chambliss and Christopher Uggen, *Men and Women of Elite Law Firms: Reevaluating Kanter's Legacy*, 25 Law & Social Inquiry 41 (2000).

8. David Wilkins and Mitu Gulati, *Why Are There So Few Black Lawyers in Corporate Firms? An Institutional Analysis*, 84 Cal. L. Rev. 493, 502 (1996).

9. Mary C. Daly, *The Structure of Legal Education and the Legal Profession, Multidiscipinary Practice, Competition, and Globalization*, 52 J. Leg. Educ. 480 (2002).

10. John E. Sebert, *The Cost and Financing of Legal Education*, 52 J. Leg. Educ. 516, 522 (2002).

11. David Wilkins and Mitu Gulati, *Reconceiving the Tournament of Lawyers*, 84 Va. L. Rev. 1581 (1998)

12. Pierre Bourdieu, *Homo Academicus* (Paris: Editions de Minuit, 1984).

13. Paul D. Carrington, *Of Law and River,* 34 J. Legal Educ. 222 (1984)

14. Gerald Frug, *McCarthyism and Critical Legal Studies,* 22 Harv. C.R.-C.L. L. Rev. 665 (1987).

15. Michael Fischl, *The Question That Killed Critical Legal Studies,* 17 Law & Social Inquiry 779 (1992).

16. Mark Tushnet, *Critical Legal Studies: A Political History,* 100 Yale L.J. 1515 (1991).

17. Reachable through Professor Karl Klare of Northeastern Law School or Professor Michael Fischl of the University of Miami Law School.

18. Reachable through the Harvard Law School Web site.

19. Ugo Mattei and Anna di Robilant, *The Art and Science of Critical Scholarship: Postmodernism and International Style in the Legal Architecture of Europe,* 75 Tul. L. Rev. 1053 (2001).

About the Contributors

Paul Carrington is Professor of Law at Duke University and sometime critic of Critical Legal Studies. He is the author of numerous articles on the history of legal education.

Peter Gabel is Director of the Institute for Spirituality and Politics and a law professor at New College of California. He was a founder of the Critical Legal Studies movement and is now Associate Editor of *Tikkun* magazine. He is the author of *The Bank Teller and Other Essays on the Politics of Meaning,* as well as some fifty articles about law, spiritual politics, and social change.

Janet Halley is Professor of Law at Harvard Law School. She is the author of *Don't: A Reader's Guide to the Military's Anti-Gay Policy* and, with Wendy Brown, edited *Left Legalism/Left Critique.* She is completing a book on the political relations between feminist, gay identity, and queer theory and politics and another book offering a left critique of sex harassment law.

Angela Harris is Professor of Law at the University of California–Berkeley (Boalt Hall). She writes widely in the area of feminist legal theory and critical race theory.

Duncan Kennedy is Carter Professor of General Jurisprudence at Harvard University School of Law. He is the author of *A Critique of Adjudication* and *Sexy Dressing, Etc.,* as well as numerous law review articles.

Donna Maeda is Associate Professor of Religious Studies at Occidental College.